AF608180

DIOCESAN CONSULTORS

DISSERTATION

SUBMITTED TO THE FACULTY OF SACRED SCIENCES AT
THE CATHOLIC UNIVERSITY OF AMERICA
IN PARTIAL FULFILLMENT OF THE REQUIREMENTS FOR
THE DEGREE OF DOCTOR IN CANON LAW.

BY THE

REV. PETER J. KLEKOTKA, S.T.B.

OF THE ARCHDIOCESE OF PHILADELPHIA.

1920.

+NIHIL OBSTAT.
THOMAS J. SHAHAN, S.T.D.
CENSOR DEPUTATUS.

CONTENTS

INTRODUCTION.

The New Code of Canon Law, which history will probably mark down as one of the most felicitous achievements of Pope Pius X, although due to his untimely death it was only promulgated by his successor, Pope Benedict XV, now gloriously reigning, has indeed revolutionized ecclesiastical discipline by introducing many salutary changes. For the Church, as a prudent legislator, while immutable in her principles, adapts herself in the details of her discipline to the needs and conditions of the particular age, or of a particular people.[1] But while the New Code does in many instances present to us new or modified legislation, it is not that which, in our judgment, gives the Code such great importance and prominence. The principal purpose of the Commission on Codification as instructed by Pope Pius X in his constitution *"Arduum sane munus"*[2] was to be *"ut universae Ecclesiae leges....ad haec usque tempora editae, lucido ordine digestae, in unum colligerentur."* After fourteen years of truly arduous labor this result has been most successfully attained. In fact one who will compare the status of Church Law as at present constituted with the puzzling condition of Canon Law before its codification, will wonder how it was that this task was not undertaken ages before and will then appreciate the New Code in its proper measure.

One result of the codification of Canon Law is that many particular and perhaps only temporary institutions, found to answer well their purpose, have now been recognized by the common law and made a part and parcel of the universal law. This applies in no small

1 "Mutantur in dies hominum mores, mutantur rerum circumstantiae, et quod uno tempore utile erat, postea inutile et quandoque perniciosum evadit. Prudentis autem Praelati est,.... se loco et tempori accomodare, etc." Bened. XIV de Syn. Dioec., V, 3, 7.

2 March 17, 1904.

measure to our own country. The United States of America, originally a missionary country, required at that time particular legislation to suit peculiar local conditions. It has however grown so rapidly that the Church here is perhaps in a healthier condition than in some of the older countries of Europe, hence as early as the year 1908[3] on the occasion of the reorganization of the Roman Curia, the Holy See found it advisable to place this country on a par with others by removing it from the jurisdiction of the Congregation of the Propagation of Faith and putting it under the common law.

This was however only one step and the process then begun has been only now completed with the promulgation of the New Code. When the new legislation went into effect on May 19th, 1918, this country became almost entirely amalgamated in the one universal law of the Church. One result of this change is that we must now look beyond the three Plenary Councils of Baltimore for our sources of law. To-day our legal guide is the one common law of the Church, the uniform discipline embodied in the New Code of Canon Law.[4] Not that the Councils of Baltimore will cease to play an important part in our national discipline, on the contrary their impress will always stand out bright in our national institutions: there is much of it that will still remain as a complement to the common law. But whenever we shall desire to find the law on a given question, it is to the Code that we must turn first of all. The enactments of the Councils will remain useful for shedding light upon the meaning of a given institution, they will also show that the condition we find ourselves in now is only the consummation of the desires of our predecessors. The work of the Fathers of the Third Plenary Council of Baltimore was "*ad ecclesiasticam disciplinam confirmandam et ad diocesium statum ita ordinandum ut propius ad, commune Ecclesiae Jus, quantum fieri possit, accedat.*"[5] That final step was now taken.

This change to the one universal law of the Church is

3 Const. "Sapienti Consilio" June 29, 1908.
4 C. 6 n. 1.
5 Litterae Apostolicae. Acta et Decreta Conc. Plen. Balt. III.

not however so revolutionary as one would perhaps at first imagine. Apart from being gradually prepared for such uniformity of law by the many constitutions that appeared during the commission's labors on codification, there is much in the New Code of Canon Law that is our own. Especially is this true of the Diocesan Consultors. A purely local and comparatively recent institution, it is now recognized and prescribed by the universal law for countries placed in circumstances similar to our own. This reveals to us the distinguishing character of the New Code. It is not so much change we find in the Code as unification; the legislator adopted for the whole what was found good for a part of the Church.

While thus making the Diocesan Consultors an universal institution, the New Code drew extensively upon the Baltimore Plenary Councils for the framework of its legislation on this point, not however without considerable modifications. This brings us to the purpose of this work. It is an humble effort to point out the new status of this important institution in the government of our dioceses. The laws affecting this institution are scattered throughout the Code. The author's task was therefore to bring them together, to compare the new with the old, for as the Code itself teaches us, it strives for the most part to retain the old discipline.[6]

While Diocesan Consultors were found in other countries besides the United States, the author has before him principally the conditions of this country. He was handicapped in his search for sources outside this country, hence points affecting other countries could only be lightly sketched, based up secondary sources. The author therefore warns the reader not to expect too much from this work. All writings on the New Code are in a certain sense pioneer works and as such their chief task is only to blaze the way that others may follow and improve their work. The writer will consider his work not undertaken in vain if he shall have interested others better equipped to follow the path here traced and expound better this, not the least of our diocesan institutions: viz: the diocesan consultors.

6 Can. 6.

CHAPTER I.

HISTORY.

The word *consultor* has received a wide acceptation in the domain of modern ecclesiastical law. Of Latin origin,[1] it signified at first the person who sought advice, the client asking counsel. From this its fundamental, passive meaning, a signification almost contrary to the original concept, was derived, viz: the active subject who gives counsel, imparts advice, or, as the English idiom would have it, the counsellor. In the former acceptation we still have the compound word, jurisconsult; but the once secondary meaning has now become the one more received and to-day when we use the word *consultor,* or its more anglicized form *counsellor,* we always bring to mind one whose task is to advise, to assist his superior in the more serious burdens of his office. Custom has introduced further distinctions, and before the promulgation of the New Code, the form *consultor* had an almost exclusive ecclesiastical acceptation, leaving to other fields such versions as *counsellor* and *councillor.* The Code, on the contrary, brought back the use of these latter forms in order to achieve the utmost possible precision, and to-day the word *consultor,* whether it be in the Latin or in derived languages, has a most unmistakable and specific meaning.

In the sharply defined sense expounded above we find the word used to signify the minor officials of the Roman Congregations[2] whose duty it is to assist the Cardinals who are the real members of the Congregation, by a preparatory study of a particular question and to offer then their advice to the Cardinals for their definitve decision. Before the promulgation of the New Code, the advisers who in most religious orders assisted the General or the

1 From the verb consulo-ere.
2 Wernz, Jus Decretalium II n. 653.

Provincial were likewise called the consultors.[3] The Code however prefers to give the members of such councils a different name, to wit: *consiliarius*[4] which term is best translated in English by *counsellor*[5] or *councillor*.[6] In this manner the Code has given the word *consultor* a more restricted and specific signification than was possessed by it in the old legislation.

The term *consultor*, while used also in connection with some of the members of the Roman Congregations, finds nevertheless its chief application and acceptance in the internal government of dioceses. But even here we find two subdivisions. Besides the consultors who assist the Bishop in the administration of the diocese as a whole and who are most properly called *diocesan consultors*, there are others to whom the term *consultors* is applied, namely, those priests whom the New Code styles *parochi consultores*[7] or, as custom has called them in this country, the *parish priest consultors*. The duties of these last can perhaps be best summarized by calling them the advisory board of appeal in the administrative removal of the so-called irremovable pastors (*parochi inamovibiles*), and in the transfer of all pastors. They are of very recent origin, having been formally introduced only by the decree *Maxima Cura* of 1910.[8]

3 Wernz, op. cit., III 696.

4 Codex Juris Canonici, can. 516 p. 1.

5 Augustine, O. S. B., A Commentary on the New Code of Canon Law, III p. 148.

6 Papi, S. J., The Government of Religious Communities. n. 100.

7 Can. 385, 2153, p. 1, 2165.

8 S. C. Consistorialis, 20 aug. 1910.

Note.—In connection with parish priest consultors we venture to point out a new use of the term consultors in a manner that may prove misleading and therefore in our judgment to be discouraged. In canons 1183-1184 of the Code there is mention of an administrative council, consisting of either clerical or lay members which may be established to assist the pastor or the rector of a church in the management of the temporal goods belonging to this particular church. In a recent dictionary of Canon Law the members of this board are styled parish consultors. The use of the term consultors could be pardoned although by analogy with can. 516 we think it would be more in conformity with the spirit of the New Code to call them counsellors. To call them however parish consultors is incorrect not only because it serves to confound them with the parochi consultores, as in fact some have loosely translated the latter phrase into parish consultors, but also because such a council could very well be established in a church that is not parochial.

With this process of elimination accomplished it will be clear now who are the *Consultors* that constitute the subject-matter of this work. They are therefore the body of priests who constitute the Bishop's council in dioceses where there is no Cathedral Chapter. They are the Bishop's advisers in the administration of the diocese as a whole and hence are called *diocesan consultors* in contradistinction to *parochi consultores* whose task as advisers to the Bishop is restricted to the limited field of removal or transfer of pastors. By some they have been styled *consultores cleri diocesani*[9] but for the sake of uniformity and precision it would be best to retain only the expression used by the Code, viz: *Consultores Diocesani.*[10]

The history of this canonical institution or the rights and duties of these diocesan consultors will not be fully understood without a brief glance at the history of cathedral chapters which this institution replaces in dioceses where for any reason the cathedral chapter does not at present exist.

It is the part of wisdom for all placed as rulers or superiors over others to seek the advice also of other men even their subordinates in matters of greater import. Although the Church is of Divine origin, her rulers nevertheless are also men, and can profit by consulting other prudent men. Hence it is that even in the time of the Apostles we find an adumbration of what subsequently developed into the modern cathedral chapter. In the first three centuries of the Church's existence there was only one church in each diocese,[11] which from the seat of the Bishop therein was called the cathedral church. The entire clergy of the diocese assembled here and in imitation of the Apostolic College formed a body consisting of twelve priests and seven deacons, called the *presbyterium,* and they assisted the Bishop not only in the administration of sacraments but also in the exercise

9 A. Van Hove in the article Hierarchy, Catholic Encyclopedia, VII-325.

10 Liber II, Caput VI.

11 Gignac, Compendium Juris Canonici, De Personis n. 473.

of jurisdiction. Often, too, the Bishop and the clergy occupied a common dwelling and led an uniform life. In the fourth century, priests were established outside the city, in the rural districts, but these were excluded from the Bishop's council and so to assist the Bishop in administration of the diocese became gradually the sole prerogative of the clergy attached to the cathedral.

Under the influence of St. Augustine who gave form to the common life of the Bishop and his clergy, this custom spread very widely, and those living in common were called canons.[12] A similar mode of life was adopted by churches other than the cathedral, giving rise thus to a distinction between the cathedral canons and canons of what were for this reason called the collegiate churches. But as the idea of common life began to languish in the tenth century, a further distinction arose between canons regular or those clerics who retained the common life in its pristine fulness and canons secular who, abandoning the original common life, retained ownership in their goods and led an individual life, but still formed one body and assembled for religious services at regular intervals. From the twelfth century on, the cathedral chapters especially acquired a great pre-eminence and were given the exclusive right of electing the Bishop and administering the vacant see, and when the see was occupied the Bishop was obliged in certain cases to seek the chapter's counsel or even consent. Moreover the chapters were firmly founded upon rich incomes which all gave rise to abuses against which the Council of Trent formulated several decrees of reformation, but the chapter always retained the right to assist the Bishop in the administration of the diocese and to rule the see in its vacancy. It is therefore the Bishop's senate, almost as some of the parliaments of modern times, without any legislative power or something like the President's Cabinet in the United States although this last does not possess any

12 For various explanations of the derivation and meaning of the term canons cf. Bargilliat, Praelectiones Juris Canonici, Ed. 30-ma; I. n. 719: Wernz, op. cit. II. n. 767 notula 4; Fanning, Cath. Enc. III-582, Article Chapter.

power in the case of a vacancy in the Presidential office.

In common with other chapters, the members of the cathedral chapter are obligated to the daily recitation of Divine Office in common, i. e., to have choir service. In recompense for this each canon has a right to a prebend, i. e., a right to the income arising from the temporal goods annexed to the title of a canon. In addition there are the daily distributions of some of the fruits of the benefices attached to the chapter, given only to those that actually attend the choir service or are considered present by a fiction of the law. From this it will be seen that the presence of a cathedral chapter in a diocese presupposes a rather advanced state of the diocese. The impossibility of having a cathedral chapter as fully organized as in the older countries of Europe, etc., is readily apparent in a diocese still under missionary conditions. True enough, the Holy See has considerably modified the ancient requirements for such countries as England, Scotland, Holland and even France after the Revolution, but with all this one will readily perceive that in countries where the Church's missionary activity falls on virgin soil, as was the case especially in the continents discovered in modern times, i. e., the two Americas and Australia, the erection of cathedral chapters in any form would require a long process of evolution and growth. To bridge this gap the institution of diocesan consultors was created with every promise of remaining a permanent institution.

Of the countries in which this institution is found today, our United States is the largest and most important, even in the ecclesiastical standards. This country was practically the first to introduce Diocesan Consultors and much of the law of the New Code on this subject is based upon the legislation provided by our three Plenary Councils of Baltimore.

It is not easy to trace the early history of our Diocesan Consultors. The territory that now comprises the United States has during the colonization period been exposed to development by different European countries carrying with them different religious life. The South and the West were developed by the French and the Spaniards: both Catholic countries,and hence gave the imprint of strong Catholic growth to their settlements. As far, therefore, as can be determined to-day these settlements adapted themselves to the common law of the Church and had their benefices, rights of patronage, and, what concerns us here most immediately, even possesed their chapters.[13] But instead of shaping the development of the Church in the remaining parts of what is now the United States, these proofs of the Church's vigor in those settlements have themselves vanished. With the victory of the Anglo-Saxon element over the French and the Spanish, the influence of the last two subsided, and their territories by a process of cession or sale were annexed finally to the young republic of the United States of America, where in those days Catholic influence was as yet small; where the exercise of Catholic worship, if not entirely proscribed, at least met with considerable difficulties at first. Under such conditions the growth of the Church in the former Spanish and French settlements took a different turn and the links with the common law of the Church in the form of benefices or chapters have almost entirely vanished.

The most advanced in point of ecclesiastical discipline were the missions established by the French, covering all the wide territory from Quebec, Canada and Newfoundland, embracing parts of what is to-day Maine and New York, down throughout the present States of Wisconsin and Michigan, the valley of the Mississippi, Louisiana and even the plains of the Far West. This immense territory, larger even than Europe, after being for a time under the jurisdiction of the Archbishop of Rouen (France), was erected into a vicariate-Apostolic in 1658 under Bishop Laval,[14] and finally in 1674 the See of Quebec was created a regular diocese, depending directly upon Rome. The Venerable Bishop Laval has himself instituted a cathedral chapter in this the first diocese in

13 Cf. Shea, History of the Catholic Church in the United States: Id. Life and Times of Archbishop Carroll. passim.

14 Cath. Enc. XII-593, Article, Quebec: Id. IX-45, Art. Laval.

the English-speaking parts of the New World.[15] This chapter continued its canonical functions until the cession of Canada to England in 1763, when, having elected Abbé Briand as Bishop, the chapter died soon after, prevented by the hostile, English government from filling its vacancies.

In the meantime the territory on both sides of the Mississippi River was undergoing its own individual development. From 1722 this territory, known as the Province of Louisiana, was[16] divided into three spiritual jurisdictions, over each of which there was a Superior, who at the same time was a vicar general of the Bishop of Quebec. The Treaty of Paris, 1763, transferred the territory east of the Mississippi River to Great Britain, and with the conclusion of the American War for Independence in 1783 this territory became part of the original United States of America. The territory west of the river, went to Spain, retaining the name of Louisiana. This brought it under the jurisdiction of the Bishop of Santiago de Cuba, which leads us into a survey of the Spanish missions.

The Spanish settlements as affecting the United States are to be studied through the colonization of Florida and Mexico, for it is from the latter country that the United States has acquired in various stages all the territory now comprised more or less in the States of Texas (annexed in 1845) ; California, Nevada, Utah and parts of Wyoming, Colorado, Arizona and New Mexico acquired in 1848 supplemented later by the Gadsden purchase in 1853. In Mexico proper ecclesiastical organization made early and rapid progress, with chapters, benefices and other marks of advanced organization and subjection to the common law of the Church. The portions, however, subsequently acquired by the United States did not for the most part pass beyond the missionary stage. Thus in Texas, originally a part of the Mexican diocese of Li-

15 Cath. Enc., XII-594b, Article Quebec: Id. III-233c, Art. Canada.

16 Cath. Enc., IX-379d, Article, Louisiana: Id. XI-6c, Art. New Orleans.

nares, at its secession from the mother country, there were so few Catholics that it was only erected into a Prefecture-Apostolic in 1840.[17] The New Mexican territory at the time of its cession to the United States was part of the diocese of Durango, which had its cathedral chapter for many years before the separation of the territory.[18] The Spanish government has indeed decreed the establishment of an episcopal see at Santa Fé as early as 1818,[19] but the Mexican War for Independence interfered, and instead, when the territory passed to the United States a vicariate-Apostolic was erected in 1850.[20] Upper and Lower California were erected into a diocese in 1840.[21] It does not appear that there was a cathedral chapter in this diocese because the administrator during the vacancy of the see after the death of the first Bishop was appointed by the bishop himself before his death.[22] Confused by the Mexican War, the Holy See appointed a successor, but as Bishop of Monterey or San Diego[23] who reached his see in 1851.

The other Spanish settlement, that of Florida, was subject from the beginning to the diocese of Santiago de Cuba, and from 1709 had resident auxiliary-bishops. Ceded by Spain to England in 1763, it nevertheless was made part of the new see of Havana in 1787. The territory was retroceded to Spain in 1783 and henceforward the ecclesiastical history of the Louisiana Province and the Floridas runs together. In 1781 an auxiliary was given to the Bishop of Santiago, to take care of this entire territory. After a brief stay under the jurisdiction of the new Bishop of Havana the Province of Louisiana and East and West Florida were erected into the see of St. Louis of New Orleans in 1793, being the second see in what now constitutes the United States. But what especially interests us, in this see we find a cathedral

17 Cath. Enc. XIV-548d, Art. Texas.
18 Shea, op. cit., IV-320.
19 Id. IV-301.
20 Id. IV-307.
21 Id. IV-351.
22 Id. IV-353.
23 Id. IV-355.

chapter erected, the first and probably the only one ever known on the territory comprising the continental United States. Unfortuntely we could not find the bull of Pius VI in the *Bullarii Romani Continuatio* but that the chapter was in very fact organized in New Orleans is evident from the historian Shea.[24] This writer, describing the promotion of the Right Reverend Penalver, the first Bishop of New Orleans to the see of Guatemala, specifically mentions that the administration of the vacant diocese then devolved on the head of the Cathedral Chapter, the Canon Thomas Hassett. Who was the other canon we have been unable to discover but before his departure for the see of Guatemala Bishop Penalver appointed Canon Hassett and Rev. Patrick Walsh as vicars-general. The latter is called by Canon Hassett the auxiliary governor of the vacant diocese, and when Canon Hassett died in 1804 Father Walsh became the sole administrator. In the meantime the Province was retroceded to France in 1800 and sold by Napoleon Bonaparte to the United States in 1803. Confusion and conflict reigned in the diocese; Canon Hassett appealed to Bishop Carroll to extend his jurisdiction over the diocese, and in fact the Propaganda issued a decree on Sept. 1, 1805, instructing Bishop Carroll to assume administration of the see of New Orleans. Bishop Carroll waited, however, until the death of Father Walsh in 1806, and then appointed Rev. John Olier to act as his vicar-general in the newly acquired province. Over the Florida portion, the Bishop of Havana again assumed jurisdiction until in 1825 the Right Reverend Michael Portier assumed charge of the new Vicariate-Apostolic of Alabama and Florida. New Orleans did not receive a new Bishop until 1818 when Dr. Dubourg took charge of the see.[25] Not improbably, therefore, the cathedral chapter may have ceased to exist in this long period of vacancy and unrest. Subsequently we find only honorary canons in the diocese, as a relic of the ancient chapter. Similar honorary

24 Id. Life and Times of Archbishop Carroll, p. 580.
25 Cath. Enc. XI-11, Art. New Orleans.

canons are found in the diocese of Natchez, Mississippi, formed out of the territory of the New Orleans diocese in 1837.[26]

Thus we have seen how in the case of the English missions, although the slowest in development, their growth was yet more persistent and constant. The thirteen colonies up to the very end of the War for Independence were subject to the Vicar-Apostolic of the London District in England. In 1784 the Sacred Congregation of the Propaganda issued a decree organizing the Church in the United States as a distinct body, with the Very Reverend John Carroll as Prefect-Apostolic. From then onward the growth was surprisingly rapid. In 1789 the see of Baltimore was erected, embracing the entire territory of the United States as then constituted. It was the first see in any part of what to-day is the continental United States, and as the country grew in extension, the influence of the English Catholic settlements overshadowed all others.

We must trace, therefore, the current of the development of ecclesiastical discipline in this country not from the French and Spanish settlements, but from the small English-speaking Catholic settlements in Maryland. The Synods and the Provincial Councils of Baltimore followed by the three great Plenary Councils directed the course of this country's ecclesiastical formation rather than the influence of the Catholic settlements in the French and Spanish colonies. But the bishoprics represented at these Baltimore Councils were not the developed and well organized dioceses of to-day. All over the United States the Church was still in its infancy, the Catholics few and far between, missions, not organized parishes, were the rule. This missionary state of affairs precluded the early establishment of anything like the cathedral chapters and out of these circumstances arose our institution of Diocesan Consultors.

The first adumbration of what we to-day call the Diocesan Consultors is to be found in the first Synod of the

26 The Official Catholic Directory.

diocese of Mobile held in 1835. As the population of the Louisiana territory rapidly increased after its purchase by the United States, Bishop Dubourg, of New Orleans, petitioned the Holy See for a division of his vast diocese. This resulted in the erection of the separate diocese of St. Louis, and after some variations also of the Vicariate-Apostolic of Alabama and the Floridas in 1825 and raised to an episcopal see in 1829.[27] The first Bishop of this see was the Right Reverend Michael Portier, ordained for and employed constantly on the missions of New Orleans. Evidently, therefore, on convoking his first Synod, he had before him the organization of the New Orleans Church with its cathedral chapter, and hence adapting the idea to the particular conditions of his diocese, he promulgated a decree in the synod establishing a council consisting of two priests appointed by the Bishop and the Vicar-general to meet once a month for the discussion of diocesan affairs. We quote this historical decree[28] no. XI. "Statutum est duos sacredotes ab Episcopo designatos una cum Vicario Generali constituere consilium episcopale et convenire qualibet secunda feria quinta cujuslibet mensis, praesente vel absente Episcopo ad discutiendam res quae ad bonum diocesis contuere possunt et investiri facultatibus in pari casu a jure concessis." We presume that by these last words Bishop Portier intended to give this council some of the rights and duties possessed by the cathedral chapters.

How soon other dioceses took up this idea, we have for the most part been unable to discover, although the language of Dr. Creagh[29] would seem to indicate the presence of a similar institution in several dioceses by the time the First Plenary Council of Baltimore was assembled. For our part we found no mention of Bishop's councils in the various directories of the clergy of the

27 Shea, op. cit., III-378.

28 Synodus Mobiliensis Prima, Notre Dame University Press, Ed. 2, 1890.

29 The Code of Canon Law and the Church in the United States. A report submitted to the First Annual Meeting of the Hierarchy, 1919.

United States antedating the year 1854. Be that as it may, the idea seemed quite satisfactory to the Fathers of the First Plenary Council of Baltimore and in one of the closing sessions of this our first great council the decree "Hortandos Episcopos"[30] was adopted by which the bishops of the country were urged to establish in their dioceses, in so far as conditions would permit, several qualified priests as their advisers in administrative matters. The reference of the decree to the custom of a monthly meeting of this council is most likely to the legislation of the already cited Mobile decree.

This advice was soon translated into action and two years after the council we find in the Metropolitan Catholic Directory of 1854 such a council of four priests established in the archdiocese of New York. In the few years following many other dioceses established the same institution; thus they are mentioned in decree n. 30 of the Hartford Synod of 1854, and in the Newark Synod of 1856 (cap. I, De Personis, c. I), in fact by the time the Second Plenary Council of Baltimore was convoked in 1866 most of the larger dioceses, and almost all of the archdioceses had their Bishop's councils, consisting then on the average of from ten to twelve members.

The Fathers of the Second Plenary Council of Baltimore supported this idea even more strongly by adding to the quotation from the First Plenary Council its own decree on the advisability of the Bishops burdened as they are with work, to share some of it with the order of priesthood so that by the united consent and vote of the two orders of priesthood and episcopacy, all be perfected for the greater glory of God.[31] After this council although no strict precept was promulgated yet in obedience to its evident spirit diocesan consultors were rapidly established in almost every diocese so that in 1874 Dr. S. B. Smith[32] was able to state that most of our Bishops if not all had their diocesan councils.

30 N. VI, in the Collectio Lacensis, III-146.
31 Concilii Plenarii Baltimorensis II Acta et Decreta, cap. V.
32 Notes on Second Plenary Council, p. 66.

Father Augustine O. S. B.[33] in commenting upon this decree of the Second Plenary Council advances the opinion that the Fathers of this Council followed the custom of other dioceses in similar condition. We do not know whether he has in mind dioceses outside the United States or not for we have been unable to find trace of such consultors in other countries before they were instituted in this country. Father Augustine O. S. B. also states that the Fathers may have been guided by the Acts of the Provincial Council of Lebanon held in 1736 for their legislation on diocesan consultors. In our study of this important council of the Maronite Church[34] we have been unable to discover any substantiation for that statement, for the different officials mentioned in caput III of the acts of this council have duties entirely different from those of diocesan consultors. In that same chapter there is indeed a reference to canons but seemingly a collegiate, not a cathedral chapter is meant. Perhaps Father Augustine O. S. B. was led to make this statement by the reference made by the Fathers of the Baltimore Council in the decree following the one on diocesan consultors.

But while the decree of the Second Plenary Council was almost universally observed by the establishment of diocesan consultors, its spirit evidently has not been quite so well translated into practice for Dr. Smith[35] exclaimed "did they exist also in reality or merely in name." This was chiefly due to the lack of definite legislation as to what were to be the rights and duties of these diocesan consultors. The Eighth Provincial Council of Baltimore[36] held in 1855 was perhaps the only one which attempted to define their duties with some precision and that only in regard to their right to present candidates for succession to the vacant see.

In this state of affairs preparations were being made for the convocation of the Third Plenary Council of Bal-

33 Op. cit. II-463.
34 Mansi, Amplissima Collectio Conciliorum, vol. 38.
35 Op. cit. p. 66.
36 N. VI: In the Collectio Lacensis vol. III.

timore. A commission of our Archbishops held conferences in 1883 at Rome with the Cardinals of the Sacred Congregation of the Propaganda and there the schema was drawn up for the agenda of the coming Third Plenary Council. Desirous of seeing the general law of the Church introduced even in the United States the Propaganda proposed at this conference to establish cathedral chapters in the United States, thus eliminating the defects in the institution of diocesan consultors. Perhaps the Fathers thought there was too great a lack of priests, or especially of ecclesiastical funds to permit the establishment of regular chapters; whatever may have been the motive, our prelates objected to the proposal, considering the time as yet inopportune.[37] To-day this is somewhat unintelligible, for the Holy See did not intend to establish other chapters than after the manner of the cathedral chapters already established in England in 1850,[38] and found also in Ireland and Holland in all of which countries they are really corporate bodies with all the rights of the cathedral chapters belonging to them by the common law as the senate of the Bishop, but with considerable modifications in the secondary duties of the cathedral chapter. As scarcely more is required from these chapters of England, etc., than that the canons recite the Terce in common and attend the conventual Mass on the day of their monthly meeting,[39] we fail to perceive any greater difficulty in instituting such chapters in the United States rather than diocesan consultors, especially as the Church in this land even at the time of the Third Plenary Council was more developed than in England.[40] Nevertheless chapters were not instituted in the United States and in their place the Cardinals recognized as an useful substitute the establishment of diocesan consultors, but the mind of the Sacred Congregation is clearly evident in that it requested that in the

37 Smith, Elements of Ecclesiastical Law, (9-th ed.) Vol. I, p. 494 note.

38 Collectio Lacensis, III-922.

39 Cath. Enc. III-584b, Art. Chapter.

40 Read Dr. Smith's article in American Catholic Quarterly Review, (Oct. 1878).

decree of the Plenary Council on diocesan consultors the establishment of cathedral chapters be not excluded. Moreover to approach more closely the ideal of the cathedral chapters, the constitution of the consultors was to be made obligatory and the consultors themselves were to be endowed with definite rights and duties, thus solving the chief source of complaint advanced against the inadequacy of diocesan consultors to fulfill the duties of a Bishop's council.

After this elaborate preparation we find the decrees of the Third Plenary Council of Baltimore on the diocesan consultors so exhaustive and definite that they have become the model for similar legislation in other lands and even form the groundwork of the legislation of the New Code in the same matter. The fundamental prescriptions of the Third Plenary Council in the matter of diocesan consultors is to be found in the Second Title of the Acts of this Council "De Personis" where an entire chapter (II) is devoted to the rights and duties of our diocesan consultors, with proper references in the other decrees of this our greatest American Council. In an introductory decree the Fathers expressed with what wisdom there have been instituted in the Church cathedral chapters to act as aids and counsellors to the burdened bishops. "Hence," continued the Fathers, "it would be very desirable that here, too, they could be shortly established, but as the present condition of our dioceses would not permit their immediate institution the Fathers decided to decree, *until otherwise provided,* the institution of diocesan consultors."[41] How patent then that this was originally meant to be only a temporary substitute.

The chief improvement noticeable in this decree over that of the preceding council is that the present council made the institution of diocesan consultors obligatory, where the Second Council only resorted to an earnest exhortation. But even more important, perhaps, is the very definite delineation of the qualities required in the consultor, their number and term of office, their mode

41 Concilii Baltimorensis Plenarii II Acta et Decreta n. 17.

of selection and removal if necessary, and finally a most definite list of their rights and duties.[42] These various points are taken up in the course of our work. Here we merely mention their general character of an unincorporated group of priests, yet endowed with definite rights and duties, so that the Bishop could not validly proceed without their advice in cases where this is required by the law.

Less than a year after the Baltimore Council followed another great Plenary Council, viz: that of Sydney, the first in Australia.[43] As the development of the Church in that land was not dissimilar to that of the Church in the United States, both being countries newly settled, it is not surprising to find the Fathers of the Sydney Council accepting for their jurisdictions the institution of diocesan consultors. Whether there were any consultors in the individual dioceses of Australia before this council we know not; at least there is no mention of them in either of the two Provincial Councils, that of Sydney in 1844 and Melbourne in 1869 which preceded the First Plenary Council of Syndey in 1885.

The decrees of the Australian Bishops on diocesan consultors, unanimously adopted at their seventh private session[44] are like those of the Baltimore Council embodied in a distinct chapter[45] but are less extensive. Substantially the provisions are the same as those enacted by the Baltimore Council, for the most, even the same wording is used. A closer imitation of the chapter is perhaps had in the decree[46] requiring their assistance at Mass in the Cathedral about twice a year at the more solemn feasts. The subsequent Second and Third Plenary Councils of Sydney reproduce these decrees without any change.

For a number of years after these two councils there seems to be a lull in the legislation concerning diocesan

42 Idem n. 17-22 inclusive.
43 Concilii Plenarii Australiensis I Acta et Decreta.
44 Idem, p. xxx.
45 Idem, n. 29-34 incl.
46 Idem, n. 31-(2).

consultors. According to Zitelli[47] the Sacred Congregation of the Propaganda never ceased to exhort the bishops in the dioceses under its jurisdiction to establish cathedral chapters, the proper senate of the Bishop in their dioceses. "Where this was impossible" continues Zitelli, "the Congregation desired that the deficiency of a chapter be supplied by the Bishop instituting a council of several missionaries, whom the Bishop should consult in the weightier affairs of the diocese and especially in the trials of clerics." The language used by Zitelli is rather general and leads us to suppose that he was referring not only to consultors in the United States and Australia but also to the existence of some at least partly similar bodies in other missionary localities.

At the very close of the last century there was held another important Plenary Council in Rome, viz: the Latin-American Council of 1899, which legislated for all the countries on the American continent south of the Rio Grande, from Mexico to Tierra del Fuego. In most of these countries, where the Church's development is to be counted in centuries, cathedral chapters have long been established. The Council however legislated for so extensive a territory that it had to take into account the new dioceses where chapters could not be immediately established and for such dioceses the institution of diocesan consultors was decreed by the Council. The decrees concerning the diocesan consultors are to be found in Titulus III caput VI of the Council.[48] They are novel in introducing the name of assessors. For the rest they are substantially the same as that of Baltimore, with some slight corrections in their form.

We have on the authority of Father Ferreres S. J. [49] that the Provincial Council of Manila[50] also passed decrees instituting diocesan consultors in the Philippine Islands and in fact Kenedy's Official Catholic Directory

47 Apparatus Juris Ecclesiastici, p. 148.
48 Concilium Plenarium Americae Latinae. 1899.
49 Institutiones Canonicae, Vol. I, n. 682.
50 Tit. 3, cap. 7, aa. 280-285.

does give several dioceses in which they are found in that Province. The writer himself however has been unable to see the acts of this council nor even to learn the exact date it assembled.

Strangely perhaps, the constitution *Sapienti Consilio* reorganizing the Roman Curia and removing the United States along with other countries from the competency of the Sacred Congregation of the Propaganda, did not by that act alone cause any change in the status of our diocesan consultors or any renewed impetus in the direction of establishing the cathedral chapters, as required by the common law. Not improbably the Holy See, considering the preparations for the promulgation of a New Code did not wish to introduce any changes so shortly before the appearance of some new legislation incident to the codification of the old laws. The discipline therefore in this regard remained practically unchanged, each country dependent upon its own particular councils for its source of law in this matter, until the appearance of the decree *Maxima Cura* of Aug. 20, 1910. Hitherto in whatever acts the Bishop was obliged to seek the advice of his consultors as determined by the various councils, he was in no wise required to follow the counsel given even if unanimous. The constitution of Pius X cited above, raised the status of consultors somewhat in that in two cases viz: in the selection of pro-synodal examiners or parish-priest consultors, and in filling their vacancies the *consent* of diocesan consultors was required. On the other hand the consultors in the United States suffered a considerable diminution in their prerogatives just before the promulgation of the New Code, when on July 25, 1916, the Sacred Consistorial Congregation revoked their right, possessed in common with the irremovable rectors, to name three candidates for appointment to a vacant see.

This brings us to the ushering in of the new legislation in the Code of Pius X. From the very beginning as is apparent from the schema of the Code, the commission on codification decided to include the institution of diocesan consultors in the new *corpus juris*. The proposed legislation of the schema is substantially retained in the Code as promulgated, with changes in the language of the canons only. The Code ushers in a new era for the diocesan consultors, due to their recognition by the common law. What their future history will be and whether they will ever be displaced by real cathedral chapters in these regions where they now obtain time alone can tell.[51]

51 It may be interesting to note that there are cathedral chapters in some of the High Episcopalian churches in this country. (Cf. Washington Star, March 25, 1920). It seems at least odd to see the traditional institution of the Catholic Church found in the separated sect, and yet apparently looked on with disfavor in the Catholic dioceses of this country.

CHAPTER II.

NATURE.

The subject-matter of this work is treated in the New Code of Canon Law in Lib. *De Personis,* the first part of which is devoted to the secular clergy as distinguished from the religious or the lay people. Under Title VIII which has to do with the power of the bishops and of those that participate in some degree in this power we find chapter VI devoted in its entirety to *Diocesan Consultors.* Here the fundamental constitution of this assemblage is specified; their particular rights and duties must be sought out throughout the rest of the Code.

In the preceding chapter we have said that the Diocesan Consultors cannot be fully understood without some knowledge of the character of a cathedral chapter. At the very outset however we must emphasize a very radical difference in their very organization. The cathedral chapter as defined by the Code itself[1] is a "*clericorum collegium* established for the purpose of more solemn worship in churches, but principally that it may assist the bishop, according to the prescriptions of particular canons, as the Bishop's senate and council, and to supply his place in the administration of a vacant see." The important word here is the term *collegium,* which is translated by college, *corporation,* society, community, company, guild or fraternity. As is clear from all these synonyms a *collegium* is an assemblage, an association of several physical persons, united by firm, precise bonds into one body politic, recognized by law as one moral person and endowed by law with rights and duties similar to that of an individual, with the capacity for succession and therefore endowed with a certain perpetuity

1 Can. 391.

of life. Of such a nature exactly is the cathedral (as well as the collegiate) chapter. It is a corporation established by proper ecclesiastical authority (in modern discipline by the Pope alone), with very definite rights and duties.

On the other hand, when treating of the diocesan consultors, the Code for some reason does not attempt to define them as a body, but for the most part speaks of them as individuals, in the plural number indeed, but by that very fact apparently showing that they do not form a strictly compact, unified body, but rather an assemblage of distinct individuals. In one case only does the Code betray in what manner it regards the diocesan consultors assembled as a body and there it calls this gathering not a *collegium* nor *societas* nor *corpus* but a *coetus consultorum dioecesanorum.*[2] Now as Father Augustine O.S.B. brings out very aptly in his commentary on this canon of the Code,[3] *coetus* signifies any assembly and cites an example of the usage of this word in Justinian's Pandects where it practically signifies a congregation assembled for the purpose of religious worship. There is however still another circumstance that adds to the general confusion. The schema of the New Code used always in connection with the diocesan consultors the expression *Capitulum consultorum dioecesanorum.*

This leads us to a somewhat difficult question for which we are obliged to confess we were unable to find a clear, certain solution. Is this *coetus consultorum* a moral person or not? In the preceding paragraphs we have indicated that this body does not appear to be a *corporation* in the strict sense. Can an assemblage which is not strictly a corporation be regarded as a moral person? The notion of a moral person in canon law is not confined to corporate bodies in their strictest sense, but is it broad enough to embrace Diocesan Consultors? Let us examine the arguments that can be advanced for either side of the question.

2 Can. 427.
3 Op. cit. II-468.

At this writing, there have appeared only two commentaries which treat of the Second Book of the New Code at any length. As the author of one of these, the Dominican Father Blat, Professor of Canon Law at the *Collegio Angelico* in Rome, distinctly calls the *coetus consultorum* a *persona moralis collegialis*. He draws this conclusion from canon 427 of the Code which assigns to this *coetus consultorum* the same rights and duties in the government of the diocese as apply to the Cathedral Chapter.[4] Reference is made to canon 100 to which we must recur for the fundamental notions on moral persons in the New Code.

Law generally, whether civil or ecclesiastical, considers the person not so much as a physical being endowed with reason and individual existence but rather as the subject of rights and duties. Such was the definition of person in the Roman law (subjectum juris capax), and in this conception it is not difficult to make the step to an artificial or moral person, which by legal fiction is a subject of rights and duties consisting of several physical persons. Ecclesiastical law, inasmuch as it also directly considers persons as subjects of rights and duties, defines a person, a member of the Catholic Church with the rights and duties attendant thereupon, all those who are baptized. In other words by baptism one becomes a member of the external ecclesiastical organization, a *subjectum ecclesiastici juris capax*. So far for the physical members of the Church, but besides these Canon Law similarly to civil law, recognizes also the moral persons as we are told explicitly by canon 99. What follows in the subsequent canon 100 is of the very essence of a moral person, be it in civil or ecclesiastical law, namely; that it be instituted by competent public authority. We scarcely need to add, that the public authority here mentioned is not any civil authority but solely the superior authorities in the Church, i. e. those who possess external jurisdiction in the Church.

4 Blat, Commentarium Textus Codicis Juris Canonici, Liber II. De Personis, p. 395.

It is this very canon 100 that constitutes the basis of the affirmative argument. The canon states that the moral persons in the Church, apart from the Holy See and the Church as such, acquire their existence, their nature as a moral person solely through the provision of Canon Law itself, (i. e of the common law viz: the Code) or by a special concession or act of a competent ecclesiastical superior, in this latter case through a formal decree. The end of an ecclesiastical moral person can only be two-fold, i. e. either religious or a charitable end.

Such ecclesiastical moral persons are again distinguished[5] into collegiate and non-collegiate bodies or as others prefer to call them, corporate and non-corporate bodies.[6] We are concerned here only with the former class, namely the collegiate moral person. The question now returns. Is our *coetus consultorum* such a collegiate moral person? Of the two contrary opinions, the one which holds that they do come under that classification is to us the preferable opinion, although we confess at the outset the grounds on which it is based are not so very conclusive.

Three elements are generally required to constitute a *collegiate* moral person First, there must be a plurality of persons and in common law the number three[7] has been chosen as the *minimum* required for the *organization* of a collegiate body. This is a heritage of the Roman law[8] and has been reduced to the pithy adage *"Tres faciunt collegium."* This element at least is fully complied with by our *coetus consultorum* for by the prescription of canon 425 p. 1 the body of consultors must number at the very least four members even in dioceses where the priests are few in number. We emphasize, this number is required for the organization of the body.

5 Can. 99.
6 Op. cit. II-24.
7 Can. 100, p. 2.
8 Dig. Lib., 50, tit. 16, de v. signif. 1. 85.

Once established as a corporation, its collective rights remain even if there be but one member left.[9]

The second element required for the constitution of a collegiate moral person might present more difficulty. It is that there be corporate rights attached not to the members individually but primarily to their collective union as such and only thus indirectly passing to the individual members. But even this requirement is fully met with in our conception of the body of diocesan consultors. For has not the assemblage as such some very definite rights in the new legislation as for example, the administration of a vacant see,[10] which right they do not possess individually but only as united in the body of diocesan consultors. It is this great innovation in the status of our consultors that leads us principally to regard the body of diocesan consultors to be from now on a real collegiate moral person. The requirement of their counsel alone, or even of their consent could very well be understood without giving the consultors any collegiate existence, as for instance no one would essay to call synodal examiners or the *parochi consultores* a collegiate moral person because their advice must be asked in the procedure of removal or transfer of pastors. We cannot imagine however the administration of a vacant see by a body of diocesan consultors, except as constituting one moral whole, namely a morál person. The Diocesan Consultors may wait for eight days[11] after the vacancy has arisen before being obliged to elect a Vicar-Capitulár or who would in our land be called the Administrator. During this time or until the Administrator is appointed by the Bishop upon whom this duty devolves in the default of consultors, they are in very fact the *Ordinary* of the diocese.[12] Unless we admit thät this right of administering the diocese as an Ordinary is vested only in the *united* body of consultors, and therefore

9 Can. 102 p. 2.
10 Can. 427, 431.
11 Can. 432 p. 1.
12 Can. 198 p. 1.

the collegiate body as such, then we would have to recognize each individual consultor as an Ordinary, which apparently would lead to absurdities. At least then in this case there is a certain definite right which can only be exercised by the assembled consultors who individually do not possess this same right.

The most serious difficulty to our assumption of consultors as a corporate body is the third requirement laid down by all laws, namely that of a legal acknowledgement. Until this legal recognition takes place, the plurality of persons have no more power than each one of the members possesses individually. This legal sanction is what is called the act of incorporation in civil law and in the latter it is generally granted in the form of a charter or a franchise. When this has been given the plurality of persons become endowed with the individuality of an artificiál body one of the most important of whose prerogatives is the capacity for perpetual existence or succession. It is not absolutely necessary however that this legal sanction come in the form of a strictly formal decree i. e. a franchise or a charter. Roman law recognized colleges formed by private persons provided this was done in conformity with certain general laws.[13] Something similar is found in Canon Law. While generally ecclesiastical corporations are formed by a formal decree,[14] yet they may be erected or perhaps it would be better to say accepted by the prescriptions of the common law itself.[15] Thus the Sacred College of Cardinals is a moral person by the prescription of the common law itself without the need of any formal decree.[16] Cathedral chapters are always instituted by a formal decree, a power reserved today to the Holy See[17] and generally these chapters are instituted simultaneously with the canonical erection of the diocese. On the other hand there is no formal decree of any kind estab-

13 Cath. Enc. IV-111d, Art. College.
14 Can. 100 p. 1.
15 Ibidem.
16 Can. 231, Blat, op. cit. II-28.
17 Can. 392.

lishing the body of diocesan consultors as such, neither in the new nor the old legislation. Both the old particular laws[18] and the New Code[19] use simply the expression *instituantur consultores dioecesani,* which does not of itself signify their establishment as a compact body but rather as individuals. We do think however that the legal sanction is supplied for our body of diocesan consultors in the other fashion, namely *ex juris praescripto* and this enfranchisement we see in canon 427, when it gives to the consultors as a body the same rights and duties as the cathedral chapter possesses in the administration of the diocese, and by that very act the Code, we think, creates the body of consultors into a real collegiate moral person.

We must admit however in all honesty that the negative side of the question does also appear strong, and extrinsically seems to have more supporters than the affirmative. As a supporter of the negative conclusion we have the only other extensive commentator on this point viz: Father Augustine O.S.B. In his commentary upon the Second Book of the Code he does not indeed explicitly state that the diocesan consultors do not form a collegiate moral person, but the inference is quite clear in several of his passages, and in one place he does indeed state that they are not at least ecclesiastical corporations in the strict sense. Thus while commenting upon canon 105 he expressly calls the readers attention to the application of the prescriptions of the canon to diocesan consultors although they *"do not as yet, like the diocesan chapter, form an ecclesiastical corporation."*[20] In another place where he discusses the desire of the Holy See that ultimately cathedral chapters be erected also in the United States he remarks "the Holy See reserves the right of changing the present boards of consultors into, say a *corporation*[21] or quasi-chapter with *corporate*[22]

18 Conc. Balt. Plen. III. Conc. Sydney. I. n. 29.
19 Can. 423.
20 Op. cit. II-35.
21 Italics are ours.
22 Italics are ours.

rights"[23] therefore implicitly denying that they are a corporation or possess corporate rights at present. When treating of canon 427 Father Augustine O.S.B. specifically points out that the term *coetus* is a wider term than *societas, collegium* or *corpus*.[24] Of considerable strength also is the observation that the body of consultors takes the place of the cathedral chapter, but that the individual consultors do not take the place of the individual canons as such. Father Augustine's next statement that for this reason the consultors do not enjoy the privileges and insignia of canons is a natural consequence. What more, Father Augustine has been so carried away by his distinction between cathedral chapters and the body of diocesan consultors, as to deny to these last the right of electing the administrator of a vacant see. His work of course, was written before the decree of the Holy See settling this point appeared.[25] Indirectly, this pronouncement of the Sacred Consistorial Congregation against the view advanced by Father Augustine tends to suggest that perhaps also his positiveness that diocesan consultors do not form a moral person is not based on very sure grounds.

The classical treatise on diocesan consultors before the promulgation of the Code was the one written by Dr. S. B. Smith for the sixth edition of his *Elements of Ecclesiastical Law*. This writer also expressly denies that the consultors have any corporate[26] existence, as having no organization as a separate body and no presiding officer or other officials of their own except the Bishop. Taunton[27] another pre-Code English writer also expressly states that they have no corporate existence. In answer to these serious objections we wish to stress the point that it is exactly the New Code that is claimed to change the nature of these diocesan consultors, and by

23 Op. cit. II-466.
24 II-468.
25 S. C. Cons., 22 feb. 1919
26 Vol. I-p. 496.
27 Law of the Church (London 1906).

the prescriptions of canon 427 endows them with a definite collegiate existence. The assertions therefore of pre-Code writers need not be conclusive any more. How too will those who prefer to deny to diocesan consultors the nature of a collegiate moral person answer the difficulty that in such a supposition there is no law in the Code to specify the procedure etc., which the diocesan consultors are to observe in the exercise of their functions which omission would be a strange oversight in the same Code that gives such important new duties to the consultors and makes their institution obligatory everywhere if the cathedral chapter be lacking. The commission on Codification consisted of so many consultors and collaborators from every part of the globe, it labored for fourteen long years and each canon appearing in the New Code was as we are told in the Preface of Cardinal Gasparri discussed four or five times if not more. Is it proper then to presume that the Commission forgot to establish any detailed regulations for the conduct of the affairs of diocesan consultors, an institution it was for the first time extending to the entire Church and therefore should have foreseen might raise doubts in countries where applied for the first time? For us it seems more in keeping with what is known about the method of the New Code to explain the apparent silence of the Code in regard to their detailed procedure etc. by the simple fact that all this is provided for in the canons regulating the procedure of collegiate moral persons in general. The Code avoids useless repetition and, as the more general prescriptions affecting all moral collegiate persons have been once laid down, it was unnecessary to repeat these prescriptions again for the particular institution of diocesan consultors if we accept the supposition that they are collegiate bodies. Perhaps one could suggest falling back upon what some writers have called *persona moralis fictitia*, viz: one that is not incorporated as an association but which only possesses the complexus of the rights of the individual members summed up together. This however is a conception not found in the

New Code which must remain our sole authentic guide in the matter of universal ecclesiastical law.

To sum up therefore, while aware of the serious objections that can be raised against this claim, we still prefer the opinion, which would recognize the body of diocesan consultors as a real collegiate moral person. We bow however in advance to any one who will clearly bring out whether the diocesan consultors are a moral person or not. We cannot escape the fact that the corporate character of a cathedral chapter is such as to give certain definite privileges and rights to the individual canons, e. g. right of precedence or of carrying a distinct, honorary robe, while we do not dare assert that our diocesan consultors *individually* have any peculiar rights or privileges. Nevertheless it might be said that this only proves that the diocesan consultors have not automatically become cathedral chapters in the strict sense of the term, perhaps even a distinction might be drawn so as to deny to the consultors the nature of an ecclesiastical corporation except in a very restricted sense but *salvo meliori judicio* we are loath to deny at least some kind of a moral collegiate personality to this institute of diocesan consultors.

The question can now be asked: are the diocesan consultors a part of the diocesan curia? The answer will depend upon the breadth of interpretation we give to this expression, i. e. whether we give it a strict narrow signification or take it in a freer, wider meaning. The New Code treats of the diocesan curia in Chapter IV of Title VIII in the Second Book,[28] a chapter entirely distinct from the one treating of diocesan consultors. In canon 363 p. 2 a list is given of the persons that belong to the diocesan curia, and in this list there is no mention made either of the cathedral chapter or of the body of diocesan consultors. The question then arises: is this list meant to be exclusive, or as the technical terminology would have it, is it an *enumeratio taxativa.* In the

28 Canons 363-390 inclusive.

opinion of a prominent canonist this list is exactly of such an exclusive character and therefore those officials who are not expressly mentioned in the canon cited cannot be said to constitute the diocesan curia in its present authentic acceptation. Logically therefore the same eminent canonist expressly states that our diocesan consultors are not a part of the diocesan curia. Before the promulgation of the Code however there was no authentic definition of the signification of the expression *diocesan curia.* The authors therefore gave it a varying interpretation. Drawing a comparison with the notion of the Roman Curia which signifies the aggregation of officials, congregations and tribunals which assist the Pope in the government of the universal Church, these writers generally defined the episcopal or diocesan curia in much the same fashion. Thus Wernz[29] calls it the complexus of those aids of the Bishop, who take part in the administration of the entire diocese, and generally reside in the episcopal city. He expressly enumerates the cathedral chapter as among the colleges of the episcopal curia. In the old legislation therefore one could *a pari* hold that the diocesan consultors also form a part of the diocesan curia inasmuch as they take the place of the senate of a Bishop. In the new discipline the diocesan consultors appear to comply with the definition of a diocesan curia laid down in canon 363 inasmuch as they are among those who assist the Bishop in the government of the entire diocese very much as the Cardinals assist the Pope in the Roman Curia. We could therefore perhaps even now speak of the diocesan consultors as members of the episcopal curia in the loose acceptation of the term but it seems that since the cathedral chapter or its substitute the body of diocesan consultors possess a certain organization of their own, the Code for this reason desired to restrict the term *diocesan curia* to the complexus of individual aids of the Bishop not otherwise organized. Practically it is not of much moment whether we hold

29 Op. cit. II-584.

the diocesan consultors as members of the diocesan curia or not for canon 364 which prescribes certain general rules to apply to all members of the diocesan curia finds its counterpart in other particular canons having reference to diocesan consultors. Thus paragraph 1 of this canon prescribing the appointments to curial offices be in writing is only a repetition of the general law already laid down in canon 159: paragraph 2. prescribing the oath of fidelity to the duties of the office is duplicated by canon 425 p. 2 which orders a similar oath for the diocesan consultors. Perhaps the only difference would be that the diocesan consultors do not seem to be bound by any definite law to observe secrecy so far as prescribed in the general rules for the performance of their duties. There is nothing however to prevent the Bishop to require such secrecy in particular instances, and in fact, speaking of the necessary convocation of those whose counsel or consent is required the Code expressly states[30] that the Superior (in our case the Bishop) can, if in his prudence he deems the situation warrants it, prescribe that the advisers promise secrecy even under oath. This makes the question, whether the diocesan consultors form a part of the diocesan curia or not a mere academic discussion of the proper usage without any practical consequence. It would be more commendable however to follow strictly the spirit of the Code and limit the expression of the diocesan curia to include only those who are actually enumerated in canon 363 p. 1 and therefore exclude the diocesan consultors from the compass of this technical term.

30 Can. 105 n. 2.

CHAPTER III.

INSTITUTION.

In our first chapter, while sketching the history of diocesan consultors, we have indicated that their institution before the promulgation of the New Code was the result of only particular legislation. The New Code however, accepts this product of peculiar circumstances and now makes it of obligation[1] upon all the dioceses where the cathedral chapter, the ultimate ideal of the Church in this respect, has for any reason been lacking in that locality. Here, therefore, we have an universal precept, of the same binding force as any other Pontifical law, perhaps even of a greater sanction because in their quinquennial reports[2] to the Holy See the Bishops are obliged to definitely state whether there is established in their dioceses the cathedral chapter or at least the body of diosesan consultors.[3] It is obligatory in all dioceses whether these be under the jurisdiction of the Sacred Congregation of the Propaganda or under the common law, for the Code makes no general exception aside from the somewhat cryptical expression *"salvis peculiaribus Apostolicae Sedis praescriptis."*[4] Of course, the Code refers only to the dioceses of the Latin Church,[5] yet some of the Eastern rites are following the example of the Western Church in this regard as, for example, the

1 Can. 423. In quibus diocesibus nondum constitui potuit restituive cathedrale canonicorum Capitulum, instituantur ab Episcopo, salvis peculiaribus Apostolicae Sedis praescriptis, consultores dioecesani, hoc est sacerdotes pietate, moribus, doctrina ac prudentia commendati.

2 Can. 340.

3 De Relationibus Dioecesanis. Nova Formula. Acta Apostolicae Sedis Vol. X, p. 487. Caput I., n. 3 (e).

4 Can. 423.

5 Can. 1.

Greek-Ruthenian diocese in the United States has five diosesan consultors.[6]

Here we must remember that the word *diocese* embraces also the abbeys and prelatures *nullius*,[7] and, therefore, the same obligation would rest per se upon them. In their case, however, diocesan consultors will seldom be necessarily instituted, for they are territories or places subject for the most part to the jurisdiction of a monastery or some other religious house, and therefore there will usually be present religious chapters of which mention is made in the Code in cap. I, Tit. X, Lib. II.[8] These religious chapters, although regulated by their own prescriptions,[9] yet will readily satisfy the requirement for a cathedral chapter as a senate of the Superior, and therefore no new cathedral chapter or a body of diocesan consultors will be strictly required. There are probably such abbeys and prelatures *nullius* which possess a secular chapter in addition to the religious chapter: such a secular chapter then follows the rules laid down in the common law. In this country we have only one strict abbey *nullius*, viz: that of the Benedictines at Belmont Abbey, North Carolina. This abbey has its own religious chapter[10] and is therefore ruled by the constitutions of the order and needs no separate body of diocesan consultors to perform the functions of a senate. While we do not know of any secular prelatures, there may be one whose superior is not a religious in the strict sense of the term but merely the head of e. g., a society of priests living in common but without vows. Brazil has several of such prelatures *nullius* but the superiors all appear to be religious and we were unable to find any clear case of a secular prelature in either the *Orbis Catholicus* (London) or the *Annuario Pontificio* (Rome). For the rest we have canon 326[11] which is only an explicitation of

6 Kenedy's Official Catholic Directory.
7 Can. 215 p. 2.
8 Can. 499-507.
9 Can. 324.
10 Official Catholic Directory.
11 Si praelatura saecularis Capitulo careat, eligantur consultores ad normam can. 423-428.

what is already contained in canon 423. In a word under the new law no real diocese or abbey or prelature *nullius* can be without a legally constituted body of advisers be they in the form of a cathedral chapter, or a body of diocesan consultors or a religious chapter.

Vicariates and Prefectures-Apostolic are not classed in canon law as dioceses and therefore do not come directly under the obligation of instituting diocesan consultors. For these, however, there is a distinct provision of a counsel somewhat similar in canon 302 but we cannot assign to the members of this council either the name or the rights and duties proper to the boards of diocesan consultors in dioceses properly so speaking. In the Vicariate-Apostolic of North Carolina, the only one remaining upon the territory of the 48 States, there is a Bishop's Council of as many as six members,[12] therefore enough to form a body of diocesan consultors, but as de facto the territory is not a diocese they cannot meet the prescriptions of the New Code certainly, and neither do we think the legislation of the Third Plenary Council of Baltimore. Hence aside from the meagre provisions of the Code for the Council of a Vicar or Prefect-Apostolic, their rights and duties must be based entirely on local statutes or particular legislation of the Holy See, and finally resort must be had to approved custom.

It is evident that this precept of instituting diocesan consultors will apply chiefly to dioceses that are still under the jurisdiction of the Sacred Congregation of the Propaganda as this congregation has precisely to deal with those regions in which ecclesiastical life has not progressed to a state of full development. But there are many, in fact, surprisingly many dioceses under the common law, or under the jurisdiction of the Congregation of Extraordinary Ecclesiastical Affairs (having relations with countries with which the Holy See has entered into a concordat) which are still without a cathedral chapter. Particularly is this true of the English-speaking countries.[13] Passing South Africa which is still merely in

12 Official Catholic Directory.
13 Orbis Catholicus. 1918.

the vicariate stage, we find no chapters in India outside the Goa Patriarchate which is principally Portuguese territory, and none in Australia which is still under the jurisdiction of the Propaganda. The situation in the United States need not be mentioned, while in Canada the Official Catholic Directory of 1920 mentions only about six dioceses with chapters. Even in Ireland while some chapters are of great antiquity, there seem to be many dioceses without chapters and in at least some of these diocesan consultors were established even before the promulgation of the Code.[14] In England and Scotland according to the *Orbis Catholicus* there is a chapter in every diocese.[15]

Stress must be laid upon the great extension of this precept, for it must be noticed that not only are the consultors to be instituted in dioceses newly organized where there never existed a cathedral chapter, but the same obligation is had in the old dioceses where for any reason the former cathedral chapter has ceased to exist, e. g., in countries that have fallen away from the Church during the Reformation. Thus in this country the cathedral chapter of Quebec has at one time ceased to exist due to the hostility of the English government, but as in that diocese the cathedral chapter has been subsequently restored the obligation of instituting consultors will not apply there. Perhaps the Scandinavian countries would offer the best example where this provision might apply, but apparently there the ecclesiastical development has not yet passed beyond the vicariate stage.

We scarcely need to pause over the observation of Father Blat O. P.[16] that if there happen to be in a diocese a chapter indeed but not only a collegiate chapter

14 Irish Ecclesisastical Record, 6-th Series, Vol. XIII, (March 1919) p. 246.

15 There is here an apparent contradiction with the statement of Taunton, denying that there are any chapters in Scotland but only diocesan consultors. This is to be explained by the date of Taunton's work published in 1906 while the Orbis Catholicus from which these facts are drawn is of the most recent date obtainable viz: 1918.

16 Op. cit. II-393.

and not a cathedral chapter, such will not answer the purpose of a Bishop's senate and hence the board of diocesan consultors must be established in that diocese as well as in any other. It is scarcely possible, however, that in any diocese there be found a collegiate chapter, which is nothing more than a college of clerics established for the purpose of a more solemn worship, performing choral service in common, without any other specific duties, while the condition of the diocese has not reached the stage of progress where a cathedral chapter could be established. If, however, it should happen, inasmuch as it is only the cathedral chapter that forms the senate of the Bishop and the diocesan consultors are an institution supplying that function of the cathedral chapter, it follows that even in such dioceses not the collegiate chapter but the diocesan consultors alone must perform the functions of legal advisers to the Bishop.

Here what may be a strictly academic question might be discussed. In these days of unrest it is not outside the range of possibilities for the Church to undergo a severe persecution at the hands of the civil authorities even in countries where ecclesiastical development is at its height. In times of such stress, as happened in Quebec, the chapter may disappear through inability to have its vacancies filled. If in addition the benefices forming the foundation of the chapter should be confiscated so that it would be impossible to restore the chapter to its previous standing, could the Bishop under such circumstances proceed on his own authority to establish diocesan consultors lest the diocese be without any legal advisers to the Bishop. We would answer decidedly in the negative. The cathedral chapter is most certainly a collegiate moral person and under the new law such moral persons do not lose their legal existence except by a definite decree of suppression from the same authority that has instituted them, namely the Holy See.[17] In the absence of such a decree of suppression a space of one hundred full years is required before the legal entity loses

17 Can. 392.

its existence.[18] Now, while the cathedral chapter retains its legal life, even though actually it is non-existent, it does not seem that another body, viz, the board of diocesan consultors, could be erected to exercise the functions of the chapter legally still alive. In our mind, under such conditions, the Holy See should be petitioned to temporarily at least suppress what we may call the charter of the cathedral chapter in order that the Bishop might then apply the faculty given him by canon 423 and establish simple diocesan consultors. Our statements here are advanced, however, with some hesitancy, for the canon just cited mentions localities where the chapter could not be restored. In our interpretation the canon does not apply here because strictly speaking there is no question of restoration as the chapter is legally still existing. Another difficulty we find in the fact that in the diocese of San Juan, Porto Rico, according to Kenedy's Official Catholic Directory there seems to be a cathedral chapter and five diocesan consultors existing simultaneously, this apparently belying our assertion that the two institutions could not coexist. We are unable to advance any satisfactory explanation, it certainly does not appear possible under the provisions of the New Code, unless by some error the cathedral chapter so spoken of is only a collegiate chapter. An authentic declaration of the Holy See upon this point would not perhaps be without some value for, although generally in persecutions the diocese itself might be suppressed and therefore the process of re-establishing religion would follow the ordinary procedure of evangelizing in missionary countries, yet as happened in New Orleans, Quebec, etc., the chapter may perish without the suppression of the diocese, while on the other hand the Bishop would be seriously inconvenienced without the presence of a legally constituted council, since its very consent is required for the validity of certain acts.

We come now to the manner in which this institution is established. Whether the body of consultors is a

18 Can. 102.

moral person or not, it is instituted not by the Holy See[19] as is the cathedral chapter, but directly by the Bishop of the diocese, in virtue of the authority now granted him by common law. In this we have one of the chief points of difference between the cathedral chapter and the body of diocesan consultors. Sometimes, indeed, the erection of a chapter is delegated by the Holy See to the Bishop as was done in Canada,[20] but the latter can never exercise this power in his own name.

It is also to be noted that they are to be instituted by the *Bishop* of the diocese, and not merely by the Ordinary of the place. The word Ordinary would include also the vicars-general and the administrator (either *sede plena* or *sede vacante,*[21]) and hence the use of the word *Episcopo* denies this power to the aforementioned persons. As far as concerns the vicars-general there is in addition the explicit canon 152 limiting the conferring of offices (and *a fortiori* their creation) to the Bishop himself, excluding definitely his vicar-general unless the Bishop grant him expressly that power. The vicar-general would of course not attempt such a step, even during an extended absence of the Bishop, but the problem might arise with the Administrator. The latter's rights, however, are more clearly expressed in canon 315. If permanently appointed, he has exactly the same rights as the residential bishops and therefore he can and is obliged to institute diocesan consultors if they be wanting. If appointed only for a time, he has scarcely more rights than the Vicar-capitular, for whom the principle is "*Sede vacante nihil innovetur.*" Neither, therefore, could the Administrator Apostolic so appointed institute the board of diocesan consultors.

This use of the word *Episcopo* instead of the word *Ordinario* does not conflict with the statement made before that the same obligation of founding boards of diocesan consultors rests upon Abbots and Prelates-*nullius*, who seldom are consecrated bishops. For them likewise

19 Can. 392.
20 Gignac op. cit. n. 494 p. 327.
21 Can. 436.

it is explicitly stated that they enjoy the same power of jurisdiction as the residential bishop.[22]

The sources or *fontes* of this legislation in the Third Plenary Council of Baltimore,[23] the First Plenary Council of Sydney,[24] and the Plenary Council of Latin- America[25] were less definite in their prescriptions as to the person instituting the board of consultors, although since they all specifically stated that the individual consultors were to be appointed by the Bishop, it was fairly clear that the institution of the board was also reserved to the Bishop. Practically this was only a confirmation that at least before the promulgation of the Code the consultors did not form a moral person, requiring a decree of erection as an organized body. From the word used by the Code *"instituantur,"* which is the same as used by the Baltimore Council,[26] it would follow that not even now is there any solemnity or special formality necessary in establishing the board of diocesan consultors. By the prescriptions of canon 423 the Bishop is obliged to do nothing else than to appoint a certain number of qualified priests to be the diocesan consultors. Each individual appointment must of course be in writing,[27] for the position of a diocesan consultor is most assuredly an ecclesiastical office in the strict sense of the term described in canon 145. But no specific written decree is required establishing the several consultors as the board of diocesan consultors. Nor do we think that this would totally destroy the foundation for our argument that the board of consultors is very likely a moral person, for they would receive this moral personality solely *ex juris praescripto,* not from the decree of the Bishop, but once established from the recognition given them by the common law. Nevertheless it would add a great deal to the value of this institution if it were solemnly established by the Bishop in a diocesan synod, as was done with the

22 Can. 323 p. 1.
23 N. 18.
24 N. 29.
25 N. 242 ff.
26 N. 18.
27 Can. 159.

first board of consultors in the diocese of Mobile, and we think, imitated by most of the other dioceses.

Some difficulty may be raised by the presence in the canon of the words *"salvis peculiaribus Apostolicae Sedis praescriptis."* No commentator so far on this canon seems to have discovered the real reason for this clause. Father Augustine O. S. B.[28] thinks it may refer to the conference held in Rome in 1883 by a commission of our archbishops making preparations for the Third Plenary Council of Baltimore.[29] In these conferences the Propaganda proposed to establish cathedral chapters in the United States, not indeed as they were known in the countries where ecclesiastical organization was at its best, but after the manner they were established in England, Ireland and Holland, where they were real corporate bodies, without, however, all the perfection or the duties of the chapters in the more developed countries. When our prelates objected to this proposal the Propaganda decided that the Third Plenary Council of Baltimore should prescribe the temporary appointment of consultors with definite rights and duties without, however, excluding the establishment of cathedral chapters at a later period when the time would be perhaps more opportune. To us this explanation of the clause does not appear very plausible. The *"praescripta Apostolicae Sedis"* must be something stronger than a mere suggestion or proposal that was advanced by the Propaganda at that conference of 1883. It might of course mean that the Holy See reserves to itself the right of disregarding the substitute institution and proceed with the erection of a real cathedral chapter whenever it would judge that action advisable. We are averse, however, to giving it this future interpretation, because the legislator, the Pope, is *supra legem* and therefore is not bound by the Code and needs no reservation to preserve his rights and powers. The Holy See could modify any prescription found in the Code and yet we do not find the phrase *salvo*

28 Op. cit. II-465.
29 Smith, op. cit. I-494 footnote.

except in a present meaning referring to rights already acquired. Father Blat O. P.[30] the only other extensive commentator on this point merely states that by this expression, *"salvis praescriptis,"* the Code retains in force any legislation previously promulgated by any Sacred Congregation whether such legislation be only different from that of the Code or even directly contrary to it. We do not know all the dioceses in which there are not as yet established cathedral chapters, and not unlikely for some among this vast number the Holy See may have made other provisions than our diocesan consultors. We must remember that after all the consultors are of a very recent origin, and that the law of the Plenary Councils of Baltimore, Sydney or Latin-America in this regard need not at all have been rigidly imitated in other countries where chapters are wanting or even where the diocesan consultors may have been established. It will be the part therefore of the Ordinaries of any diocese still lacking the cathedral chapter or its substitute, the diocesan consultors, to investigate whether there be, perhaps, some peculiar provisions of the Holy See for their own particular territory, exempting them from the general obligation of establishing the diocesan consultors. It will certainly not, however, exempt any possible diocese of the United States or Latin-America or Australia for in all these countries the establishment of diocesan consultors was prescribed years before the promulgation of the New Code. What is the prescription of the Provincial Council of Manila mentiond by Ferreres[31] in this regard we do not know. A Plenary Council was held in Quebec in 1909 but to date its decrees have not been published or promulgated. Perhaps in these countries an explanation of this reservation would be found, there is nothing in the *Collectanea S. Congregations de Propaganda Fide*[32] that would seem to shed any light on the question. A similar reservation is found in the schema of the Code, i. e., the draft of the Code which was

30 Op. cit. II-393.
31 Institutiones Canonicae, I, p. 242 n. 682, notes.
32 Romae, Editio nova (1907).

sent out to the Bishops. Unable therefore to arrive at any satisfactory explanation of this reservation we must leave to others more proficient to favor us with the key to this secret.

Here an explanation may be given of the note placed to this canon. As any reader of Cardinal Gasparri's preface to the Code will know, these notes referred to in different canons are properly speaking the sources of the law from which the present legislation is drawn or in which at least the subject of the present legislation was in some way mentioned. The sources indicated are always from the supreme Papal authority, either from the *Corpus Juris* or the Ecumenical Councils or at least the general decrees or particular responses of the Roman Congregations. Councils which are not of the universal Church, even though their decrees may have been reproduced in the Code are not given. The first reference in our note is to the response of the Sacred Consistorial Congregation which had for its purpose the solution of several doubts arising out of the promulgation of the decree *Maxima Cura*[33] by the same Congregation. A question[34] was asked of the Congregation whether the diocesan consultors whose consent, as was originally established by the decree *Maxima Cura,* was required in the election of pro-synodal examiners or parish priest consultors were the same persons as the parish-priest consultors mentioned in the decree itself. The answer was of course negative and it was explained that the diocesan consultors are those who take the place of the cathedral chapter in those dioceses where for any reason these could not as yet be erected. This was the first universal pronouncement of the Holy See on the nature of the diocesan consultors. Up to that date their constitution was to be found only in the decrees of the Plenary or Provincial Councils approved indeed by the Holy See but not promulgated by it as pontificial laws.

The second reference is a declaration of the same Con-

33 Aug. 20, 1910, A.A. S.
34 N. 9.

gregation of the Consistorial on the eligibility of the Vicar-General as a diocesan consultor. As this will be taken up *ex professo* in Chapter V of our work we postpone our remarks until our treatment of the point there.

It sometimes happens that two or more dioceses instead of being altogether suppressed are united to other dioceses. This union may be of several kinds similarly as may take place with any other benefice.[35] If the union is not suppressive the individual dioceses retain their former characteristics with the sole exception that they are always administered by one and the same bishop. In such a case the individual dioceses retain their individual chapters. *A pari* therefore, if such an union should occur with dioceses which do not possess cathedral chapters, in their case the individual dioceses must possess their own particular boards of diocesan consultors. As long as they are not suppressed such dioceses come under the provisions of canon 423 and therefore obliged to the establishment of boards of diocesan consultors. There is no immediate prospect of such united sees here in the United States.

35 Cf. can. 1419 ff.

CHAPTER IV.

APPOINTMENT.

Diocesan consultors are appointed by the Bishop.[1] Our remarks in the preceding chapter about the meaning here of the term "bishop" apply with equal force in the matter of their appointment. As affecting the United States a slight change will be noticed between the law of the Baltimore Councils and the New Code. The Third Plenary Council of Baltimore[2] did likewise prescribe the appointment of the consultors by the Bishop but required that half of their number be named by the Bishop indeed but out of nine names proposed by the diocesan clergy actually engaged in the care of souls. By common practice this was interpreted to refer only to the secular clergy, thus excluding the religious of any form even if they were given charge of a parish.[3] It was considered more desirable that this proposition take place in the diocesan synod,[4] but as synods have been of rather rare frequency in the United States practice has developed the system of proposing these names in writing[5] through letters sent by the individual priests to the Bishop's office, a custom which as Dr. Baart[6] pointed out as early as 1898 has rendered the law more or less nugatory The spirit of this legislation was that those candidates be elected in whom the diocesan clergy have shown the most confidence by giving them the highest number of votes. Actually however as each priest presented nine names and as the Bishop was free to choose any one whose name was suggested even though he possess but

1 Can. 424: "Consultores nominat Episcopus, firmo praescripto can. 426.'

2 N. 19.

3 Meehan in the Am. Eccl. Rev. XLV-491. Still there were frequent exceptions.

4 Baart, Legal Formulary, p. 43 (New York 1898).

5 Cath. Enc. IV-323, Article "Diocesan Consultors."

6 Op. cit. p. 43.

one vote, one will see that the Bishop had almost an unlimited field to choose from. The sole limitation was that the name be proposed by some one of the diocesan clergy. We must however always remember that the actual appointment or nomination was in the hands of the Bishop in the law of Baltimore as it is now in the New Code.

The councils of the other countries viz: Australia and Latin America left the appointment entirely with the Bishop, without even the formality of a proposition by the clergy and this method has now been adopted by the New Code. The question now arises, can the method prescribed by the Third Plenary Council of Baltimore be still followed in the United States, even after the promulgation of the New Code as if it were a particular prescription *praeter legem universalem* and not *contra.* In answering we must draw a distinction. The decrees of the Third Plenary Council of Baltimore which are the foundation of this method of procedure are not pontifical laws but only episcopal laws, which indeed by reason of their conciliar enactment cannot be abrogated by the individual bishops, but this does not change the nature of these laws. The revision of the Council's acts by the Sacred Congregation of the Propaganda Fide or even their approval *in forma communi* (which however is doubted)[7] does in no wise impart to them the character of pontifical laws. Hence the prescriptions of the Baltimore Council can not under any interpretation be included in the clause *"salvis peculiaribus Apostolicae Sedis praescriptis"* of canon 423. But is it something *praeter Codicem* and therefore not abrogated in virtue of canon 6 n. 1.? To this we answer in the negative. The limitation of the right of free nomination by the Bishop as set down in canon 424, to a set of names proposed by the diocesan clergy even though it may be ever so slight a restriction is nevertheless a modification, an infringement of the rights given the Bishop by canon 424 and hence is to be regarded as *contra legem universalem* and

7 Smith, op. cit. p. 78 footnote.

consequently absolutely abrogated. But this simply means that the *right* of proposition is abrogated: the New Code does in no wise render such procedure illegal. On the contrary it might be commendable in our mind to retain the traditional practice in this country as providing a most excellent method for the Bishop to discover which priests possess the greatest respect and confidence in the diocese But as the Bishop would not in any way be bound to choose any of those proposed, neither is he bound to make half of the selection entirely of his own choice: if the Bishop should therefore choose to receive suggestions from his clergy he would do well to accept these proposals for all of his consultors and not only for the half as formerly prescribed by the Baltimore Council. Such a procedure would likewise be in keeping with the spirit of the Code as shown in the manner of appointment of simple canons in a cathedral chapter, which must be done *audito Capitulo*.[8] It would be well then, if the proposal by the clergy be not practicable that the Bishop at least consult his former consultors before appointing new consultors. In very fact such a provision was laid down in the Australian Synods.[9] We are speaking here of course of selecting members for a new term, not to fill an unexpired vacancy. Whatever procedure then the Bishop might choose to follow in accordance with the previous custom in his locality it is not to be taken to limit the Bishop's right to free and entirely unhampered appointment.

The change in the method of appointment disposes of most of the questions hitherto mooted in various volumes of the American Ecclesiastical Review in regard to the proposition by the clergy, as to the persons proposing these names,[10] or of the Bishop passing over the names because of their previous appointment as irremovable rectors,[11] or whether undue agitation by the priests that

8 Can. 403.
9 Cf. First Australian Plen. Council n. 31-3 (e).
10 American Ecclesiastical Review. XLV-491.
11 Ibid. XV-545.

their favorites obtain the highest number of votes could be classed as simony (answered in the negative because it was not election but only proposition)[12] or finally of the defective legislation in the manner of selection. With the right of nomination now vested entirely in the Bishop all these questions are no longer of interest.

Some modification of this unhampered and free right of the Bishop to appoint his consultors is to be noted when a vacancy occurs before the individual consultor's term of office has expired or when their term lapses during a vacancy of the see, as we are expressly reminded by the canon we have been treating here viz: can. 424. In canon 426 p. 3 we are told[13] that if during the three year term of office the position of one of the consultors should become vacant, for whatever cause this may be, whether by resignation properly accepted or by death or even by removal observing the equities of law, the vacancy is filled by the Bishop but only to complete the unexpired term and before appointment the Bishop must take counsel of the remaining consultors, otherwise the appointment is utterly invalid.[14] Of the taking of counsel we shall speak more later. This provision is exactly the same as in the Baltimore law[15] and was repeated verbatim in the Sydney[16] and Latin-American Plenary Councils.

If the vacancy in a similar manner occurs while the see itself is vacant then by paragraph 5 of the same canon[17] it is the Vicar-capitular who appoints the consultor who is to fill the unexpired term but only with the *con-*

12 Ibid. XXXIII-638.

13 Par. 3 "Deficiente, quavis de causa, aliquo consultore intra triennium, Episcopus alium de consillio ceterorum consultorum substituat, isque in officio maneat usque ad expletum idem triennium."

14 Can. 105.

15 N. 21.

16 N. 34.

17 Par. 5 can. 426 "Si, sede vacante, aliquis consultor moriatur vel renuntiet, Viccarius Capitularis, de consensu aliorum consultorum, alium nominet, qui tamen, ut munere, sede plena, fungatur, indiget novi Episcopi confirmatione."

sent of the other consultors and subject to the confirmation by the new Bishop as regards continuing in duty after the new bishop has taken formal possession of the diocese. This paragraph is entirely new as none of the Plenary Councils mentioned here have any provision to fill a vacancy occuring during the vacancy of the see itself. It is a most wise legislation for without some similar provision it would not be impossible for all the consultors, especially if their number be limited, to die or otherwise relinquish office and leave the administrator of the diocese without any legal advisers at a time when the diocese may be most in need of precisely such a body, for if the Bishop requires the advice of others, all the more is this true of the temporary administrator.

There are a few important differences in this canon to be stressed as compared with the filling of a vacancy *sede plena.* In the first place the vacancy can only occur by the death or the resignation of the consultor. During the vacancy of the see therefore no consultor can be per se removed against his will, even though he has lapsed into some crime. This last statement however is to be considered in the light of canon 188 enumerating several cases where the office is declared vacant *ipso jure* by tacit resignation. Moreover there are numerous crimes e. g. joining the masons[18] for which the Ordinary and hence even the Vicar-capitular must remove the guilty party from office. Of this however we shall speak more under our remarks about removal from office (Chapter VII). Here we must only note that the Code does not permit the Vicar-capitular to fill the vacancy if it should occur in any other way than by death or resignation (including tacit resignation). Practically of course it could seldom happen that a vacancy would occur through crime because most of these cases would require a formal judicial trial to establish the guilt and then only could the Vicar-capitular as the Ordinary inflict the *poena ferendae sententiae* viz: the privation from office. The

18 Can. 2336.

cases where such a punishment is to be applied will be found in the Index of the Code under the word "Privatio".

Some confusion is caused by the use in the canon of the word "Vicar-capitular". This name is given to the cleric who is elected by the cathedral chapter[19] during the vacancy of the see (as also *sede impedito,*[20]*)* to govern the diocese in the place of the chapter upon which the administration of the see originally devolves. The diocesan consultors as they take the place of the cathedral chapter in all that pertains to the government of the diocese[21] are also obliged to elect during the vacancy of a see, one who will in their stead govern the diocese. It has been the custom in this country to call the priests who governed the vacant see the Administrator and the writers after the Code retain this usage for the person who is to be elected for this purpose by the diocesan consultors. As the body of diocesan consultors will only be found where there is no chapter the person having to do with the filling of the vacant position of a consultor as mentioned in this paragraph of the canon is not the Vicar-capitular strictly so called with us but the Administrator of the diocese. It would seem therefore that the Code should not have used the term Vicar-capitular in this connection. Not impossibly however the Code desires that even the person chosen by the diocesan consultors be called the Vicar-capitular, leaving the term "administrator" solely to the priest who is not elected by the body of diocesan consultors or the cathedral chapter, but who is designated by the metropolitan, or any other bishop to whom this power has been given by the special disposition of the Holy See.[22] This would be slightly confirmed by the usage suggested by the schema of the New Code, which would have called the body of consultors *capitulum consultorum dioecesanorum,*

19 Can. 432.
20 Can. 429 p. 3.
21 Can. 427.
22 Can. 431 p. 2.

which expression accepted it would be quite reasonable to call the Administrator chosen by such a *capitulum consultorum* the Vicar-capitular, for the Administrator as truly rules the diocese in the name of the body of consultors as the person chosen by the chapter rules the diocese in its name. We need only to mention that if the Administrator be a person chosen according to the prescriptions of canon 431 p. 2 he in virtue of the same canon possesses the same rights and duties as the Vicar-capitular, and therefore he too has the power of nominating the substitute consultor in the vacancy of which we have been speaking.

The most important point of difference however between appointment by the Bishop and appointment by the Vicar-capitular (Administrator) is that the latter requires the *consent* of the remaining consultors. This is for the validity of the act and is regulated by canons 101 and 105. As we shall speak more of consent later, we need only mention here that a majority vote is sufficient. Attention is drawn to the provision of the same canon 426 that this substitute continues in position only during the vacancy of the see, unlike the other consultors who continue to the end of their term and if that should elapse they may retain their position for six months after the accession of the new bishop unless the latter before that time has either confirmed them or appointed new consultors. Concluding this chapter we may repeat that the appointment must be in writing.[23] A form that could be commendably used, with some changes necessitated by the New Code is given by Fr. Baart.[24]

23 Can. 159.
24 Op. cit. p. 49.

CHAPTER V.

QUALITIES.

The position of a diocesan consultor is an ecclesiastical office in the strict sense of the term as laid down in canon 145, and therefore the fundamental prescriptions established in Title IV *"De officiis ecclesiasticis"* have their proportionate application to diocesan consultors. Of particular importance are chapter I, on canonical provision, (omitting the articles II and III on election and postulation) and chapter II on the loss of ecclesiastical offices.

Canon 153[1] reminds us that the cleric who is to be appointed to any given office should possess the qualities required by law for that particular position, and his fitness for it may be even tested by an examination.[2] Among several available candidates, all possessing the required qualities, he is to be chosen who all things considered is the best man for the position.[3] This is only natural equity but it is a principle that should never be lost sight of. Attention also might be drawn to canon 154 which prohibits the collation of any office upon the relatives of the person who resigned or was deprived of that office.

To receive any ecclesiastical office the candidate must possess certain qualities which might be styled negative, as e. g. freedom from excommunication,[4] interdict[5] or suspension[6] and from infamy[7] whether of law or of

1 Par. 1—"Ad vacans officium promovendus debet esse clericus, iis qualitatibus praeditus, quae a jure communi vel particulari aut a lege fundationis ad idem officium requiruntur."

2 Can. 149.

3 Can. 153 par. 2—"Assumatur, omnibus perpensis, magis idoneus sine ulla personarum acceptione." Cf. also Can. 130 p. 2.

4 Can. 2265 p. 1 n. 2—and p. 2.

5 Can. 2275 n. 3.

6 Can. 2283.

7 Can. 2293-2294.

fact. There are several crimes, to which is attached the penalty of *infamia juris*, as for example, to those participating in a duel.[8] The list of such crimes is to be found in the Index of the Code under the word "*infamia*". As regards excommunication, interdict and suspension the prohibition of bestowing an office upon such is only for liceity, but after a declaratory or condemnatory sentence such a person cannot *validly* obtain an ecclesiastical office.

More important however are the positive qualities as it could scarcely happen that a Superior would knowingly confer an ecclesiastical office upon a person belonging to one of the above mentioned classes. The positive qualities required in a diocesan consultor are not so very exacting as in the case of some of the other ecclesiastical offices, yet as they are to be the advisers of a bishop they must be representative priests and excel in all the sacerdotal virtues. Canon 423 states that they should be priests noted *(commendati)* for piety, good morals, knowledge and prudence. This is almost a restatement of the law of the Baltimore Council[9] the decree of which expressed the requirements at somewhat greater length, mentioning in addition solicitude for the salvation of souls, experience with men and their affairs and of course diligence in the observance of the prescriptions of the general law as well as of the diocesan statutes. The Plenary Council of Latin America[10] expects the consultors to be preeminent in virtue and in maturity (of the mind rather than physical maturity) and in whom the Bishop could place full trust. As the consultors take the place of canons of the cathedral chapter it may be well to study too the requirements laid down for them in canon 404 which should have at least a directive force in the choice of diocesan consultors. The canon referred to instructs the Bishop to appoint to canonries, all other things being equal, those who have obtained an ecclesias-

8 Can. 2351 p. 2.
9 N. 18.
10 N. 243.

tical degree in a Catholic university, or who have done commendable work in their ministry or have been especially successful in the so-called junior clergy examination.

To these wise and clear provisions of the Code and of the various councils we need add no commentary. The question can now be raised, can a religious, particularly one having charge of a parish, be appointed a consultor? Actually there are dioceses in this country now in which at least some of the consultors are religious,[11] can such an action be retained in the light ofthe New Code? Unfortunately the Code does not give us a direct or a definite answer. There is however a canon[12] which states that religious cannot be promoted without a special authorization from the Holy See, to any office that is incompatible with the religious state.[13] Although this leaves the question almost where it was yet it seems to indicate that the spirit of the law is against any such appointment of a religious to the position of a diocesan consultor. Then there is the serious difficulty as to the time or the duration of the stay of the religious in the diocese for the Superior of the religious can transfer him to another diocese without any other formality than that of notifying the Bishop of his intended action if the religious is a pastor.[14] This question has been discussed at some length in the *American Ecclesiastical Review.*[15] As the writer of the article in the Review points out, the function of the diocesan consultor being to safeguard by his advice the special interests of the Church in his particular diocese, it presupposes not only a general fitness as possession of good priestly qualities, but also that the consultor be a permanent part of the diocese, subject directly and immediately to the Bishop of the diocese and

11 Cf. The Official Catholic Directory.

12 Can. 626 "Religiosus nequit, sine Sedis Apostolicae auctoritate, ad....officia...... quae cum statu religioso componi non possint."

13 As defined in Can. 487-488.

14 Can. 454 p. 5.

15 Vol. XLI-474.

consequently intimately interested in all that concerns the welfare of the diocese. Since even the parish priests who are religious may be recalled *ad nutum* by their Superior after a simple notification[16] those that have no charge of a parish are subject even more strongly to this possibility of transfer to another diocese regardless of the requirements of any special service they may have undertaken to perform on the diocese as accepting the position of a diocesan consultor. Of considerable force also is the objection that such a religious diocesan consultor would always remain subject to the will of his Superior in the religion, who might himself be entirely out of touch or harmony with the needs of the diocesan clergy. Besides, humanly speaking, the special interests of religious communities may not always allow their members to note the local needs of dioceson government and to pledge their aid in the same manner as the secular clergy is permanently pledged (in the title of ordination *servitii ecclesiae*) to the service of the same diocese and bishop. All this however is merely concerning the expediency of selecting a religious as a consultor. If actually so appointed, for example after an arrangement with the Superior of the religious priest, or by reason of diocesan necessity or peculiar local conditions, the nomination will certainly be valid. Comparison can be made here with the position of the parish-priest consultor instituted by the decree *Maxima Cura.*[17] A question was asked of the Sacred Consistorial Congregation,[18] could the Ordinary appoint a regular as a synodal examiner or the parish-priest consultor[19] and the answer given was in the affirmative, provided however in the case of an appointment to the position of a parish-priest consultor that the regular be himself a pastor but this follows from the very nature of the work of a parish-priest consultor.

16 Can. 454 p. 5.
17 S. C. Consist., 20 aug. 1910.
18 3 oct. 1910, ad 4.
19 The response does not indeed qualify the word consultor but as it is in its entirety an interpretation of the Maxima Cura it is clear that the reference is to the parish-priest consultor.

There is no substantial reason why the spirit of this response could not be applied also to the choice of a religious for a diocesan consultor, i. e. there is no legal objection to such an appointment but the response does not in any way change the objective inexpediency of at least regularly appointing religious to the function of a diocesan consultor.

While considering this series of interpretations of the decree *Maxima Cura* let us note also the response to Dubium no. 8, could one and the same person be at the same time a synodal examiner and a parish-priest consultor. While the answer given was also affirmative it carried with it the advice that generally it is not expedient for one and the same person to hold several offices. The same principle should be before us in reference to diocesan consultors. In one diocese the diocesan consultors are also the synodal examiners of the diocese. While local conditions may warrant such accumulation of duties in the same person it should not be accepted as a general rule.

Another question agitated in the *American Ecclesiastical Review*[20] was, could the Bishop appoint those outside his own diocese to act as his diocesan consultors. A similar question has been taken up by the Sacred Consistorial Congregation[21] in reference to synodal examiners and parish-priest consultors. The answer in either case was in the affirmative for the reason that in the appointment of officials the law looks primarily to the fitness of the candidate and only indirectly or accidentally to the locality of the candidate. So far from requiring that the officials be from the diocese in which they are to hold an office it was the law before the promulgation of the New Code that the Vicar-general for example be chosen from outside the diocese. In the response cited the answer was indeed in the affirmative but shows distinctly that it is to be regarded as an odious exception requiring some just cause, such as would the more readily arise in

20 Vol. XLVIII-463.
21 3 oct. 1910.

small dioceses, where priests possessing the necessary requirements are few. There is nothing in the New Code to restrict this privilege, yet account must be taken of the difference between the work of a diocesan consultor and that of a parish-priest consultor or even synodal examiners. Parish-priest consultors need only be called by the Bishop when a pastor files objections to his transfer[22] or when an irremovable rector whose administrative removal is under consideration takes recourse against the Bishop's decree of removal. One will readily understand therefore that the occasions where parish-priest consultors will be called upon to exercise their functions will be few and rare indeed. The same would apply in a scarcely lesser degree to the work of a synodal examiner, whose duties[23] are almost similar to those of the parish-priest consultor. On the other hand, especially under the new law, occasions where the diocesan consultors must be heard by the Bishop are numerous and may come up even quite unexpectedly. Besides the extern priest would hardly possess the knowledge of diocesan conditions one would expect in the legal adviser of the Bishop, nor would he answer very well to the requirements of canon 425 p. 1 that the diocesan consultor live in the episcopal city or close by. All things considered therefore while the appointment of an outside priest as a diocesan consultor would not seem to be clearly invalid, yet it should not be resorted to unless for some extraordinary reasons.

A question that has received a great deal of attention on the pages of the *American Ecclesiastical Review* and which finally brought forth an official declaration from Rome was, whether the Vicar-general could at the same time be appointed a diocesan consultor. This question was moved as early as the year 1894.[24] The answer then given in the Review was that the Vicar-general was ipso facto a member of the Bishop's council because

22 Can. 2165, 2153.
23 Cf. passim Tit. XXVII-XXXI. Also Can. 389.
24 Vol. X-452.

juridically he is almost the same person as the Bishop and by reason of this official rank entitled to presence at the official or formal councils of the Bishop. The same question was later taken up in the *Legal Formulary* of Dr. Baart.[25] Quoting a response of the Sacred Congregation of the Propaganda in 1886 Dr. Baart defends the choice of a Vicar-general as a diocesan consultor even if he be the *consultor natus* of the Bishop, provided only the vicars-general be in the minority. This brought forth a renewed discussion of the point at considerable length in the *Ecclesiastical Review*.[26] The writer of that article while admitting the custom to obtain in many dioceses of the United States of either appointing the Vicar-general as a diocesan consultor or considering him such ipso facto, denies to the Vicar-general any right of suffrage in the meetings of the diocesan consultor and states that this was "according to established law." This allusion of the writer we do not understand, for to our knowledge there was no written law or official pronouncement on that phase of the question at that early date. Of interest however is the answer of the Cardinal Prefect of the Propaganda cited by the writer. Cardinal Simeoni held that the two offices were essentially distinct and for this reason should be discharged by different persons and hence his decision was "Negative vel saltem non expedire." When the Archbishop of New York wrote the Cardinal Prefect of the Propaganda that his Vicars-general knew the diocese very well and hence their advice in matters upon which the law requires the hearing of diocesan consultors would be of no little value and importance. The Propaganda moved by these considerations answered "Tolerari posse, modo tres saltem alii consultores habeantur" which however was only a provision for a particular case but required that the Vicars-general be in the minority and this is the point to be remembered.

The custom however of appointing the Vicar-general

25 P. 44.
26 Vol. XX-636.

one of the diocesan consultors continued. Subsequently, among the dubia interpreted by the Sacred Consistorial Congregation in the decree *Maxima Cura* was one on the question whether the Vicar-general could be appointed a synodal examiner and the answer given was "Non expedire."[27] This could be taken to express the mind of the Holy See on the similar question of the inexpediency of normally appointing the Vicar-general a diocesan consultor. In the end however a specific declaration came from the same Sacred Consistorial Congregation[28] which ought to settle the question once for all. In this declaration the Cardinals of the Congregation specify as the reason for their decision the consideration that in the dioceses of the United States (to which the response was alone addressed although it can be taken to have directive force elsewhere) the diocesan consultors take the place of the canons of a cathedral chapter and the college of consultors takes the place of the cathedral chapter as the senate of the Bishop. As there was no prohibition in the common law against the Vicar-general being included among the members of the cathedral chapter (and on this there is no change in the New Code)[29] the Cardinals concluded that as a general rule it could not be prohibited in the United States that the Vicar-general be appointed one of the body of diocesan consultors.

Note however the qualification. If in any particular case the number of the consultors be very small (e. g. only two) whether it be out of custom or for any other cause, then the choice of a Vicar-general as a diocesan consultor would be inexpedient and inequitable, and in such circumstances either one who is not a consultor is to be chosen a Vicar-general or the number of consultors is to be increased.

The spirit of this declaration seems to have been observed quite well in the United States since its promul-

27 3 oct. 1910, ad 6.
28 27 feb. 1914, A. A. S. VI-III.
29 Cf. Can. 421 p. 1 n. 3.

gation. In at least half of the dioceses of the United States the Vicar-general is also a diocesan consultor but, as in almost all of these dioceses the number of diocesan consultors is six or at least four there is no prejudice to the spirit of the declaration. It seems that in only one diocese is the number of consultors limited to two among whom is also the Vicar-general.

The New Code does not in any way abrogate the permission granted by this declaration of the Sacred Consistorial Congregation. Whatever then may have been the objections of the Holy See to the appointment of the Vicar-general as a diocesan consultor where their number is small, to-day they may be appointed without the least objection provided only the prescriptions of the Code requiring at least four consultors be observed. If there be only four consultors and one of their number a Vicar-general then there are still three other members or a majority sufficient to dispose of the objection in cases of consent to be given by the diocesan consultors that the Vicar-general and the Bishop are one juridically. If however there be two Vicars-general among the diocesan consultors, as it sometimes happens, then the total number of consultors must be at least five so as to have at least a majority of one who are not Vicars-general. With these precautions observed, the presence of the Vicar-general among the diocesan consultors may perhaps be even recommended for it cannot be denied that next to the Bishop he probably will be best acquainted with the diocese and therefore best qualified to be among the Bishop's advisers.

Here attention may be drawn to the peculiar wording of the declaration. It calls the board of diocesan consultors a *collegium* and appears to compare individual consultors with the individual canons of a cathedral chapter, apart from the rights they possess as a body. Such language favors the contention that the body of diocesan consultors is a moral person.[30]

30 Cf. Chapter II.

Another question which may present some difficulty is whether an ex-religious i. e. one legitimately saecularized or dispensed could be appointed a diocesan consultor. The Sacred Congregation of the Religious issued a decree dated June 15, 1909 which to check the desire of religious to obtain the indult of saecularization specified that every such indult or dispensation carries with it a prohibition among others to hold or receive any office in the Cathedral Church or in the episcopal curia. With this decree in mind a writer in the *American Ecclesiastical Review*[31] answered a question raised whether an ex-religious could become a diocesan consultor in the negative requiring for this purpose a specific, Apostolic indult. The answer was most probably correct in the old legislation but what of the same question after the promulgation of the Code. The decree cited is embodied almost verbatim in canon 642. The difficulty arises from the fact that it seems almost certain that diocesan consultors are not members of the diocesan curia[32] as we have already pointed out in Chapter II of this work.[33] As we are in the presence of a restrictive legislation we are to give it a strict interpretation in accordance with canon 19. It is our opinion therefore, *salvo meliori judicio*, that the appointment of an ex-religious to the position of a diocesan consultor without a new and specific indult from the Holy See would not necessarily be invalid. It is clear however that it remains against the spirit if not the letter of the law. The *ratio legis* as given in the dispositive part of the decree cited above obtains as much, if not even more, with the position of a diocesan consultor as with the offices mentioned in the canon and as the Regulae Juris had it *"Ubi eadem juris ratio eadem debet esse juris dispositio"*. The same is brought out by comparison with the canons of the cathedral chapter. An ex-religious could not become a member of a cathedral chapter because the canonicate is most

31 LV-562.
32 Can. 363 p. 2.
33 In fine.

generally a secular benefice in the cathedral church from which such an ex-religious is excluded. In the light of these circumstances the appointment of an ex-religious to the position of a diocesan consultor is at least to be discouraged.

We need only mention here the former discussion whether an irremovable pastor should be appointed a diocesan consultor.[34] The basis of the objection was the former privilege of our irremovable rectors in common with the diocesan consultors of presenting three names for appointment to the vacant bishopric. In the desire that the electoral college in the case be as large as possible, it being the common opinion that one holding the two offices should not cast two ballots some bishops have refused to appoint irremovable rectors as diocesan consultors, even after their commendation by the clergy Since the Sacred Consistorial Congregation by its decree of July 25, 1916 took away the power from both the diocesan consultors and irremovable rectors this question for us in the United States becomes entirely unimportant for outside of these reasons the two honors are in no way incompatible. As far however as we are aware the old system of presenting the names for a vacant see is still in force in Australia.[35] As the two functions are not in themselves incompatible we prefer to accept the opinion expressed in a response to a somewhat similar question in the *Amer. Ecclesiastical Review*,[36] that the desire to increase the electoral capacity should not act against the choice of an irremovable pastor as a diocesan consultor. As the choice however rests freely with the Bishop there will not be the same source of misunderstanding as prompted the discussion cited in the Review.

In closing our remarks in this chapter we may mention a discussion taken up in the Ecclesiastical Review as to the eligibility of a young man as a diocesan consultor.[37]

34 XV-431, 545.
35 Cath. Enc. II-585b.: Irish Eccles. Record 5S. XIII-246.
36 XV-546.
37 LVI-534.

The Code does not set down any age requirement for the position of a diocesan consultor therefore in accordance with the oft quoted axiom *"Ubi lex non distinguit nec nos distinguere debemus."* The only diocesan office for which the Code prescribes an age requirement outside the Bishop himself is that of the Vicar-general The Code sets the age of thirty as the minimum for a Vicar-general, and if, the spirit of the Latin-American legislation be worthy of imitation, this age too could be set down as a reasonable minimum before we may expect to find in the candidate the maturity spoken of by the Latin America Council.[38] If anything, the position of a diocesan consultor calls for an older man than that of a Vicar-general because in the Vicar-general acquaintance with the diocese is not necessary since he may even be chosen from outside but the diocesan consultors in a sense represent the voice of the diocesan clergy and how could they perform this task well except after a long life among the clergy of the diocese. Let us however leave it to the Bishop to judge at what age one becomes a fit candidate for the position of his adviser. Prudence is the most desirable quality, and advanced age generally can be regarded to be more prudent than the young.

38 N. 243.

CHAPTER VI.

NUMBER, OATH AND TERM OF OFFICE.

Of the number that should be appointed diocesan consultors little need be said. As a general rule canon 425, p. 1,[1] states they should be at least six in number. By far the greatest part of the dioceses of the United States contain this very number of consultors. This number, however, is not laid down by the Code as the maximum, but as the minimum, at least in dioceses of ordinary size. Not only are the bishops therefore not prevented from appointing a larger board, but the Code itself recommends this by using the word "saltem." The number of diocesan consultors could well be in some measure proportionate to the number of priests in the diocese. If a diocese of perhaps 250 priests has six consultors there is no reason why a diocese containing 500 priests should not have also twice as many consultors. Strange to say, in the beginning of their history these bishops' councils were always large and numbered twelve or more consultors.[2] What has brought about the almost universal limitation to six we do not know. Perhaps the decree of the Third Plenary Council of Baltimore[3] by its prescription that they number six or at least four or if even this be impossible at least two, had an indirect effect of causing the number six to be regarded as more or less the maximum. More explicit was the First Plenary Synod of Sydney[4] establishing that for the sake of uniformity there be six in each diocese if possible, with the same exceptions as established by the Baltimore Council. The

1 "Consultores dioecesani numero sint saltem sex; in dioecesibus ubi pauci sint sacerdotes saltem quatuor."

2 Cf. e. g. the Catholic Directory of 1866.

3 N. 18.

4 N. 30.

Latin-American Council established the number four and in smaller dioceses at least the number two.[5]

As the body of diocesan consultors holds the place of a cathedral chapter, their number should in some way resemble the number common to chapters. While these in smaller dioceses number only six or seven canons, in the greater they number as high as twelve or more members. Thus the Archdiocese of Quebec[6] has twelve canons, the diocese of Trois-Riviers (also in Canada) has eleven. The Primatial chapter of Armagh, in Ireland, numbers as many as nineteen canons. But what surprises us the most is that even in England where the Church is no more flourishing than in the United States, the Metropolitan Chapter of Westminster numbers eighteen canons. In the United States, on the other hand, the largest number of consultors found is nine, and in only four dioceses is the number above six. We think, therefore, the spirit of the Church's legislation and even of our former traditions would be better complied with if the number of consultors in the larger sees be raised to about twelve for instance. Uniformity is indeed a virtue, but it, too, should be adapted to particular conditions. If all the archdiocesan board of consultors should number about twelve members, we would still have the desirable uniformity and at the same time come closer to the spirit of the legislation in regards to the number to be contained in the Bishop's senate.

But while there is no limitation to the maximum number of consultors, there is a very positive check as to the minimum that may be chosen. The Code says that ordinarily six should be the number appointed. There are, however, dioceses where this requirement would be somewhat burdensome. Thus there is a diocese in the western part of the United States that numbers little over thirty priests and of these only seven live in the episcopal city. For such dioceses, therefore, where the territory may be very extensive, but the number few, the law

5 N. 243.

6 These figures are taken from the Official Catholic Directory for 1919.

makes an exception and permits that in such dioceses the consultors number only four. But in no diocese no matter what its condition can there be less than four consultors. The prescription, therefore, of the Baltimore,[7] and Latin-American[8] councils permitting the number in extreme circumstances to be only two, must now be corrected as opposed to the prescriptions of canon 425.[9] Scarcely three or four of the dioceses in the United States are affected by this changed requirement.

We advance this opinion with considerable hesitation but we think if the number of consultors does not answer the requirements of canon 424 then neither do they come under the provisions of canon 427 and therefore would not possess the powers now assigned by common law to diocesan consultors. We have in mind a case where the number of consultors was never raised to the number required by the Code, for if they once meet the requirements and subsequently the number is lessened by a natural vacancy, then we think in comparison with other collegiate bodies their rights once acquired remain, even if there be but one member left.[10] Three are necessary to constitute a moral person[11] and even in Prefectures-Apostolic the Superior of the mission is obliged to constitute a council of at least three priests. Perhaps if the consultors number at least three they would still come under the provisions of canon 427 but we rather doubt whether two could be given the important rights and duties now assigned to diocesan consultors. A pronouncement from the Holy See on this point might not be unwelcome because, while the New Code insists on the number four as the very minimum, there may occur cases where this prescription might be neglected, and then the validity of certain acts of these consultors might be questioned. We cannot deny probability to the opinion that even two consultors would constitute a *coetus*

7 N. 18.
8 N. 243.
9 Can. 6, n. 1.
10 Can. 102 p. 2.
11 Can. 100 p. 2.

consultorum as mentioned in canon 427 and therefore would possess the rights established there. While therefore it must be insisted upon that the number of consultors be raised everywhere to four as the minimum required by the Code yet we would not venture to call the acts performed by a board of consultors of smaller numbers as absolutely and certainly invalid. Perhaps others could decide this question more authoritatively.

A further requirement of the New Code, which is altogether new for us in the United States and which, as Father Augustine, O. S. B., aptly points out,[12] betrays a leaning towards the cathedral chapter is that the diocesan consultors live in the episcopal city or at least not too far away from it. In a country, however, like the United States, where the railway connections are on the whole very good, this requirement will cause little difficulty. This prescription had its origin in the Latin-American Council[13] (in some of the countries of Latin-America due to the hostility of the government there are few dioceses and those that are created are for this reason so extensive that travel for some sections of the dioceses to their episcopal cities would require days if not weeks). The law is taken almost verbatim from this great council. As the diocesan consultors are the Bishop's senate exactly as the cathedral chapter it is expected that they be within convenient reach of the city when called by the Bishop, especially since their duties have now been increased. Too great a distance from the city might seriously hinder the exercise of some of their duties, when a prompt answer would be required by the Bishop. As the promptness of attendance is the sole *ratio legis* it is not so much the absolute distance that is to be taken into account as rather the relative capacity of reaching the episcopal city in a reasonable time. Those acquainted with our large cities know that sometimes one living fifty miles away from the city can reach a given point in the city sooner than some

12 Op. cit. II-466.
13 N. 243.

of the citizens residing within the geographical boundaries of the city but in some of its inaccessible parts.

Somewhat new, at least new so far as the existence of a specific written law is concerned[14] is the second paragraph of the canon we are now considering.[15] Before the consultors undertake the duties of their office they must take an oath promising faithful service in their position without any respect or acceptation of persons. None of the former particular legislations required this oath of office from diocesan consultors although Dr. Baart[16] requires a similar oath as prescribed by the common law of the Church for all public offices in the Church. In the New Code it is an obligation attached to most ecclesiastical offices and while there is considerable doubt that the position of a consultor is an ecclesiastical office in the strict sense of the term there is the specific prescription of this canon requiring the diocesan consultors to take an oath of office.

Some difficulty may be found by reason of the failure of the Code to specify before whom this oath is to be taken. For some reason which he does not state Father Blat O. P.[17] thinks the official to receive these oaths would be perhaps the chancellor. More probable in our mind is the interpretation of Father Augustine[18] who, drawing upon canon 1406 for comparison, thinks that the person receiving the consultors' profession of faith should also receive their oath of office. Such an interpretation would be quite in line with the provisions of the New Code itself which in canon 18 instructs us in cases of doubt to seek out the hidden meaning of some obscure prescription by recurring to parallel legislation in the Code. One of such parallel provisions is found in canon 364 p. 2 where the members of the diocesan curia

14 Baart, op. cit. p. 45.

15 Can. 425 p. 2 "Antequam munus huiusmodi suscipiant, jus jurandum interponant de officio fideliter exsequendo sine ulla acceptione personarum."

16 Loc. cit.

17 Op. cit. p. 394.

18 Op. cit. II-467.

(as defined strictly in a preceding canon) are instructed to take their oath of office before the Bishop. This would seem at first glance to exclude the Vicar-general but considering canon 368 which gives the Vicar-general the same power as the Bishop possesses unless specifically excepted we do not think it would be against the letter of the law for the Vicar-general to receive the oath from the diocesan curia and *a pari* from the diocesan consultors. The comparison however drawn by Father Augustine permits us to draw an even more liberal interpretation. If the consultors can make their profession of faith before the Ordinary or his delegate there is no reason why on the same occasion they would not take their oath of office before the Ordinary or his delegate. Of course the latter would have to be appointed by the Bishop especially *ad hoc*.[19] Here one should carefully note canon 1316 p. 2. Any oath required by the New Code must be taken personally, so much so that an oath by proxy would apart from being illicit be altogether invalid.

As the requirement of an oath of office is at least new in its more specific and definite prescription so too somewhat new or at least more certain and definite now is the obligation of the diocesan consultors to make a profession of faith before undertaking the exercise of their duties. Already Pope Pius IV in his constitution "*In Sacrosancta*" (a. 1564) prescribed the profession of faith to be made among others by all those who are promoted to an ecclesiastical office.[20] The Plenary Councils of Baltimore, Sydney and Latin-America do not make any reference to this profession of faith in connection with diocesan consultors. Whether such a profession of faith was exacted from the diocesan consultors the writer is not aware. Dr. Baart[21] said they should have made the profession of faith but Smith in his *Elements*[22]

19 Cf. can. 200.
20 Wernz, op. cit. III-14.
21 Op. cit. p. 45.
22 N. 661.

exempted the rectors of the United States from this obligation which leads us to doubt whether he thought diocesan consultors should have made this profession. Only recently Pope Pius in his constitution *"Sacrorum Antistitum"*[23] establishing certain precautions against the error of modernism prescribed[24] that both the profession of faith and the so-called oath against modernism be required of all members of the episcopal curia. If not in the letter of the law at least in the mind of the *Motu Proprio* it seemed to be clear that the diocesan consultors were to be included under both obligations. To-day there is no doubt that the diocesan consultors are obliged at least to make the profession of faith, for they are expressly mentioned as among those who are required to make the profession of faith. We think also that they are obliged to take the additional oath against modernism, from the fact that it might be said to be included in the expression *"secundum formulam a Sede Apostolica probatam"* as prescribed in the first words of the canon we are treating. There is also the declaration of the Sacred Congregation of the Sacred Office of March 22, 1918 in which it is explained that as the oath against modernism was meant to be only a safeguard against the evils of the day and hence more or less a mere temporary legislation, it could not be very well explicitly included in the New Code which is a body of law to stand for some time perhaps to be unchanged in substance at least for ages, but until the Holy See decrees otherwise the oath and the other laws against modernism mentioned in the declaration are to be understood as still binding. It is true the declaration does not add any explicit mention that the diocesan consultors should be included under its provisions but as it is meant to retain the spirit of Motu Proprio *"Sacrorum Antistitum"* we think that the oath should be exacted from the diocesan consultors even now. If consultors can no longer be classed among the members of the diocesan curia in the strict sense of the term,

23 A. A. S. Ii-655.
24 Id. p. 668.

there remains their parity with the canons who are explicitly included among those who are obliged to take this oath. If we deny this obligation to diocesan consultors then they will be practically the only ones holding any diocesan position who would not be bound by the obligation of taking the oath against modernism which would be indeed a peculiar oversight of the law in which we are to be guided by the axiom *"Ubi eadem juris ratio eadem debet esse juris dispositio."*

The profession of faith must be made before the Ordinary of the place and therefore it is clear that it includes the Vicar-general and the Vicar capitular or the Administrator. No difficulty need arise as to the required presence of the other consultors when only one vacancy is being filled. But who are the *"alii consultores"* before whom those appointed to the position must make their profession of faith when all the members of the board have completed their term of office and for the next term only new ones are appointed. Are these new nominees to make their profession of faith in the presence of the former consultors or does it mean that each individual member of the new board of consultors makes his profession not alone indeed but in the presence of the others likewise newly appointed to the position. *Salvo meliori judicio* we prefer to take the latter view, for the old consultors cease to be such on the third anniversary of their appointment, whereas the new consultors may be considered to have gained possession of their office as soon as they have received their appointment in writing (or any other clear manner), unless a date be specified on which their duties begin, but even then it does not seem that the oath of office is necessary to gain canonical possession of the office or position. In interpreting a law we are always to look to the intention of the legislator[25] and it seems to us in this case that the purpose of the law is equally well attained if the profession be made in the presence of those who are only about to begin their term

25 Can. 18.

of office. We do not however mean to exclude the presence of the old consultors, and we think it would add to the solemnity of the occasion if the oath of office and the profession of faith be made by each individual consultor in the presence of both the retiring and the newly elected members of the board of diocesan consultors. Before leaving this point attention must be drawn to canon 1407 requiring that the profession of faith be made in person and not before a layman, otherwise the person does not satisfy the obligation incumbent upon him. The last canon of this section[26] reprobates any contrary custom and therefore betrays to us how anxious is the legislator that the prescription of this title be most faithfully observed. No other formality is necessary to take formal possession of the position of the diocesan consultor. Whatever particular customs there may be in the manner of inducting diocesan consultors into their duties may be most laudably retained, if none are known the method prescribed by Dr. Baart[27] may well be made use of viz: through the imposition of the biretta by the Bishop.

We come now to the discussion of the consultors' term of office. According to canon 426[28] their work is to be for three years. In this we have about the most important difference in the new law between the individual consultor and the individual canon of the cathedral chapter whom he represets, and whose place he takes. The office of a canon by reason of the benefice most generally attached to it is of its very nature a life appointment, from which he cannot be removed except for causes specified in law and with the observance of certain formalities. Our diocesan consultors on the other hand are appointed only for three years, when that time elapses they automatically lose their office or position and to continue at their duties they require an express and new confirmation. By some this short term of office is not regarded as satisfactory. Thus Dr. Baart[29] said that it has prov-

26 Can. 1408.
27 Op. cit. p. 49.
28 P. 1 "Officium consultorum est ad triennium."
29 Op. cit. p. 44.

en itself detrimental in that it does not help to obtain the purpose of the institution of diocesan consulors, who, fearing they will not be reappointed at the end of their term may not be as honest in their advice as perhaps might be expected of them. While there may be some weight to Dr. Baart's criticism there is a good deal to state in favor of a short term else the New Code would not retain it.

The duration of the diocesan consultors' term of office was first prescribed by the Third Plenary Council of Baltimore[30] and following its footsteps both the Sydney[31] and the Latin-American[32] Councils, all prescribe the term of office to be for three years. The New Code has retained this term without the slightest change. This period of three years is to be computed in accordance with the general rules laid down in title III of the First Book of the Code and especially canon 34 p. 3. Therefore if the Bishop appoints a new board of consultors whose term of office is to begin for example on the 15th of August 1920 their term would expire automatically on the midnight of 15th of August 1923, i. e., unless they be confirmed for a new term, the diocesan consultors in the case cited could not validly perform any act of their office on any part of the said August the 15th, 1923.[33]

When this triennial term elapses, naturally, since the consultors are no longer validly such, the bishop must either appoint new members in their place or confirm the same members for another triennial term.[34] When the consultors thus end their term of office the Bishop is entirely free to select either the same men or make an altogether different choice. The desirable thing of course, ordinarily speaking, would be that the same consultors be retained term after term, or at least that a ma-

30 N. 21.
31 N. 34.
32 N. 244.
33 Can. 34 p. 3 n. 2.
34 Can. 426 p. 2 "Exacto triennio, Episcopus vel alios in eorum locum substituat, vel eosdem ad aliud triennium confirmet, quod idem servetur singulis trienniis."

jor portion of them be re-appointed so that the Bishop and the diocese could profit al the more by their maturer judgment, based upon greater experience. Such an action would be also more in keeping with the life term of the canons' function in the cathedral chapter whom we must always remember the diocesan consultors are meant to represent and replace and therefore may meritoriously imitate them so far as possible in their function as the legal advisers of the Bishop. Yet there is no necessity to criticise absolutely the three year limit, for there well may be occasions when a change in the personnel of the board of diocesan consultors would be of advantage for the smoother and more efficient administration of the diocese. This might especially be true when a new bishop is appointed to the vacant see and we can well understand the wisdom of the Church in not insisting upon too long a term of office for the consultors, especially as these have not the choral duties of the cathedral chapter. The objection that the short term may retard the consultors' freedom in expressing their honest opinion on a given question if this should be contrary to the desires of the Bishop would not have so much weight where the number of consultors is not too small and as regards questions involving the giving of consent that should be settled by a secret vote and therefore there should be no especial fear of the Bishop's displeasure.

As confirmation of the old consultors for a new term is in no wise different from their new appointment, all the rules laid down in the preceding chapter on the appointment of consultors apply equally to the confirmation of the old consultors and therefore this too should be in writing. We scarcely need to point out that the triennial term continues even if a new bishop is appointed to the see as consultors once appointed retain their position until either their term expires or for some extraordinary reasons they are removed during their triennial term of office, always remembering the consultors are not removable ad nutum.

The triennial term of office suffers some modifications

in certain particular instances. As the board of consultors is meant to be a more or less homogeneous body it is not composed of members whose terms of office would elapse at varying intervals but it is so constituted that the triennial term elapses for the entire board at one and the same time. From this it readily appears that if ever for any reason a vacancy should occur during this triennial term of office to replace the retiring consultor only a substitute can be appointed to serve not three years but only the remaining portion of the former consultor's triennial term. It is very much like the procedure observed in the legislative bodies of the United States where vacancies are filled by men who are only to occupy the seat for the unexpired portion of the senator's or representative's term.

The old particular legislation of Baltimore,[35] Sydney[36] and Latin-American Councils,.[37] had no specific provision on this point. They all spoke of appointing a new consultor in the place of the one retiring for any reason aond like the Code (in fact the words are the same) required counsel of the remaining members but no explicit mention was made of the term of office. What the new law however prescribes clearly and explicitly seems to have been contained in the old more or less implicitly, and therefore this would not seem to constitute a substantial innovation.

More important is the modification in the term of office that takes place when the term expires during the vacancy of the see. It is clear that the appointment to so important a position as that of the diocesan consultors should not be made by the temporary administrator of the diocese and therefore the Fathers of the Third Plenary Council of Baltimore prescribed that in the case of such a vacancy the consultors continue to hold their position even after the expiration of their three year term and do not lose then their office until the accession of the

35 N. 21.
36 N. 34.
37 N. 244.

new bishop or rather until the new bishop within six months of his accession appoints new consultors or confirms the old.[38] The First Plenary Council of Sydney[39] and the Latin-American Council[40] used exactly the same words, with the sole difference that the Latin-American Council prescribed six months of grace from the time of taking canonical possession of the diocese not as the other two councils specified not so logically, six months from the time of consecration. The New Code[41] retains substantially the same prescription as the Latin-American council. For whatever reason then the see may be vacant (not simply "impedita") the consultors do not lose their position but remain in secure possession of their office until the new bishop is not only appointed or has taken canonical possession of his see but until the new bishop within the six months allowed him either reappoints the old or appoints new consultors. Canonical possession of the see is accomplished by the presentation of the Apostolic briefs containing the appointment of the Bishop to the see in question, to the board of diocesan consultors in this country either personally or even by proxy. But once this formality has been observed the newly appointed bishop obtains full jurisdiction in his diocese and can exercise it even if he be not as yet consecrated, on the contrary a bishop already consecrated would have no power of jurisdiction in the diocese for which he is appointed until he does actually take canonical possession of it in the manner prescribed in the New Code. The language therefore of Baltimore and Sydney Councils in this regard was misleading and hence too the Code establishes as the time of grace, six months from the time the new bishop has entered into the possession of his see.

The consultors therefore do not lose their position dur-

38 N. 21.
39 N. 34.
40 N. 244.
41 Can. 426 p. 4. "Cum vero triennium excidisse contigerit vacante sede episcopali, consultores in officio maneant usque ad accessum novi Episcopi, qui intra sex menses ab inita possessione providere debet ad normam huius canonis."

ing the vacancy[42] nor even at the moment of the accession of the new bishop but remain in their office until the bishop takes contrary action i. e. appoints new consultors if he does not confirm the old. The sole exception is that the Bishop is obliged to take some definite action in regard to the consultors remaining in office within six months from his own accession and if it should happen that at the end of that time the Bishop has still failed to take action in regard to his consultors, we think, *salvo meliori judicio,* that the consultors' term of office then automatically expires just as the ordinary triennial term expires sede plena the moment the three calendar years are accomplished. At first glance it would appear that the consultors lose their position the moment that the new Bishop takes possession of his see but comparison with the rest of this canon shows that this cannot be the meaning of the paragraph. The wording of the following paragraph clearly indicates by contrast that a substitute consultor appointed during the vacancy of the see cannot continue to exercise his duties after the see has been filled without obtaining immediate confirmation of the new bishop: the body of consultors therefore must remain longer in office and that is until the new bishop takes definite action in the manner already explained. Moreover the entire spirit of the canon shows the intention of the legislator to be that there be no time when the diocese would find itself without a board of legal advisers: viz: its diocesan consultors, nay even more there is to be no time when even individual vacancies are to remain unfilled.

The last modification of the triennial term is the appointment of the consultor during a vacancy of the see who as already mentioned, does not continue to exercise his duties after the accession of the new bishop except with his express confirmation. In other words he does not remain in office as long as the other consultors even if their term of office has scarcely begun when the va-

42 Cf. Can. 183 p. 2.

cancy occurred, for, unless he be confirmed by the new bishop he ceases to be a consultor. In still other words this means simply that such a consultor's term of office automatically expires the very moment the new bishop takes possession of the see. Such a substitute consultor can and should be present at the presentation of the Apostolic Letters of the Bishop to the board of diocesan consultors but the moment this action has been completed this substitute is to all intents and purposes no longer a consultor, for the necessary confirmation by the new bishop is nothing else but a new appointment.

In the *American Ecclesiastical Review* of 1899[43] a few questions were raised in connection with this triennial term of the diocesan consultors which however can all be readily answered. The point of the questions was when did the former see become vacant in the transfer of its bishop to another see. To-day we have the explicit provision of canon 194 that in case of a transfer the office from which a priest is transferred becomes vacant only the moment when the transferred cleric has taken formal possession of the new office, unless the law in a particular instance ordains otherwise. But in the case of a transfer of a bishop we have precisely such a divergent, particular prescription in canon 430 in which it is definitely established that the former see from which the bishop is being transferred becomes vacant the moment that the Bishop receives certain notice of his transfer. After the receipt of this notice and until he takes possession of the see to which he has been transferred he retains in the former diocese only the power of the Vicar-capitular. The answer therefore given in the Review will remain substantially correct even to-day. If the bishop has received only unofficial notice e. g. through a cable message from some friend at Rome and the consultors' triennial term has expired, the bishop still retains full powers in the diocese and can appoint new consultors, which indeed would be quite desirable in the circumstances lest

43 Vol. XXVI-293.

the diocese be left without a board of consultors at the very time when they are most required viz: during the vacancy of the see. The transferred bishop retains his full powers therefore until he receives a *certain* notice of his transfer. These words are interpreted by Father Augustine O. S. B.[44] to mean authentic notice or official notice: by Father Blat O. P.[45] they are taken to mean any document worthy of belief. Such a document we think will generally be in the form of an official message from the Apostolic Delegate to the bishop concerned. Incidentally this possibility shows how important it is that the confirmation of the old or the appointment of the new consultors should never be delayed. In the case supposed, if the Bishop were suddenly confronted with a telegram from the Apostolic Delegate notifying him of his transfer, his consultors even if their term had lapsed only the day before, are unable to retain their positions nor is the Bishop able to appoint new members and the diocese would find itself without a board of consultors. An even worse situation could arise in the case of a sudden death of the Bishop. The administration of the vacant diocese could in either case be provided for by the metropolitan or the senior suffragan bishop as the case may be who in such a case have the power and the duty to appoint the administrator. But neither the Administrator in the absence of at least some consultors nor any other superior below the Holy See could appoint a board of consultors and thus he might be seriously handicapped where the law requires their counsel or consent. In the supposition the only recourse would be to the Holy See (the Sacred Congregation of the Council) to obtain the faculty to appoint at least a temporary board of consultors. Since the principle however is "*Sede vacante nihil innovetur*[46] this difficulty would become serious only in the case of a prolonged vacancy.

Casual reading of canon 430 p. 2. would seem to indicate that what we have just said is incorrect because the

44 Op. cit. II-478.
45 Op. cit. II-401.
46 Can. 439.

appointment to offices is excepted in that paragraph from the acts which remain valid despite the vacancy. In answer we wish to stress the first paragraph of the same canon which states that in the case of transfer the see becomes vacant when this act is formally intimated to the Bishop. Here then is a change from the old law. Formerly the see was declared vacant the moment the transfer was announced in the Consistory by the Pope:[47] now the see becomes vacant when the bishop receives notice of this act in accordance with canon 192 for the term *"intimata"* in the paragraph qualifies not only the word *"privatione"* but also the word *"translatione"*, to which it is joined by the strong conjunctive particle *"ac"*. What the second paragraph establishes refers rather to the case where the Bishop dies and so affects the powers of the Vicar-general, also it seems to apply to the Bishop who resigned his see and the resignation was accepted In the latter case the Bishop appears to lose all his powers in the diocese the moment the Holy See accepts his resignation although canon 190 would even here require the notification of the acceptance of the resignation. Most likely therefore the exception made in the second paragraph in regard to the collation of offices must refer only to the Vicar-general having for such actions a *"mandatum speciale"*[48] which expires with the loss of jurisdiction in the *"mandans"*.[49] As regards removal of a bishop from his see this privation follows the same rules as translation in the necessity of an authentic notification. To summarize therefore all acts of the bishop and therefore even appointment of new consultors are valid until the authentic notification of the acceptance of a resignation or of the transfer or privation properly reaches the Bishop. In practice however there will scarcely be opportunity to apply these rules because as it is the custom of the Holy See to notify the Bishops of the action taken in their case by cable through the

47 Wernz, op. cit. II-527.
48 Can. 152.
49 Augustine, op. cit. II-477.

Apostolic Delegate there will scarcely be time for any contingencies here described to arise.

More practical is the question what is to be done if the triennial term expires after the bishop's appointment to another diocese but before he has formerly left the former diocese to take possession of the new see. From what has already been said it is clear that the former see is juridically vacant, the moment the bishop has received authentic notification of his transfer and therefore canon 426 p. 4 finds application here with the result that the consultors remain in office until the accession and the action of the new bishop. Although vacant the administration of the see is already provided for by canon 430 p. 2 *ipso facto* creating the transferred bishop the Vicar-capitular of the diocese. The board of consultors does not therefore take over the administration of the diocese for the election of its own Vicar-capitular until the former bishop leaves the diocese and then the consultors proceed to the election of a new Vicar-capitular in accordance with the prescriptions of canon 443.

CHAPTER VII.

REMOVAL, PRECEDENCE, TITLE, ETC.

Once appointed the diocesan consultor is irremovable during his term of office except in so far as this is permitted by the general legislation for the loss of offices in Lib. II, tit. IV, cap. II of the New Code, which must govern the case of diocesan consultors equally as well as any other ecclesiastical office. In other words the diocesan consultors are not removable *ad nutum.* The five ways in which one may lose an ecclesiastical office are according to canon 183 by resignation, privation, removal, transfer and the lapse of the term of office. Of the last we have already treated in the preceding chapter. (Chap. VI). Concerning transfer there is not much to be said, it will scarcely find application in the case of diocesan consultors, for the rest any just cause will suffice if it takes place with the consent of the person concerned; if not it follows the rules laid down for privation. Between privation and ordinary removal *(remotio, amotio)* the Code does not attempt to define the difference but privation generally seems to signify removal on account of some demerit[1]. while *amotio* is removal rather for the good of the people concerned than a form of punishment. The New Code appears to use the terms almost indiscriminately, for us it will be sufficient to remember that there can be no removal of a diocesan consultor simply *ad nutum Episcopi.*

The first method of losing an ecclesiastical office is by resignation. In connection with this it is sufficient to indicate in general the doctrine to be found in the Code in canons 184-191. Apart from a specific prohibition any one can resign[2] but to be valid it must be an act that

1 Blat, op. cit. II-122.
2 Can. 184.

is free from unjust fear, error etc.,[3] it must be in writing or before two witnesses,[4] must be accepted by the Bishop in our case[5] and does not take effect until the one resigning is notified of its acceptance by the competent superior.[6] Of some importance is canon 188 prescribing tacit resignation, which would be of especial value during the vacancy of a see for as we have already stated in chapter IV it seems that theVicar-capitular can only appoint substitute consultors in place of those that have died or resigned. If therefore a diocesan consultor *sede vacante* should for example, apostatize from the Catholic faith, the Vicar-capitular can proceed directly to the appointment of a new consultor with the consent of the remaining consultors just as he would proceed if the consultor in question has resigned.

There remains for fuller consideration privation and ordinary removal. The first principle to be observed here is the prescription of canon 428[7] namely that consultors be not removed during their term of office except for just cause and with the counsel of the other consultors. Subordinate to this we have the general principles laid down in canon 192 for the privation of any ecclesiastical office and hence also holding true of the privation of diocesan consultors from their office. We must remember too the existence of an *ipso facto*[8] privation for certain classes of offences, as for example an *excommunicátus vitandus*[9] loses all his ecclesiastical offices without any further formality. Again there are offences for which the law prescribes a privation as a punishment *ferendae sententiae* and in those cases the Ordinary including therefore even the Vicar-capitular, is obliged to proceed with the privation as e. g. in the offences

3 Can. 185.
4 Can. 186.
5 Can. 187.
6 Can. 190.
7 "Durante munere, consultores ne removeantur, nisi ob justam causam ac de consilio ceterorum consultorum."
8 Cf. index of the Code under the term "Privatio."
9 Can. 2266.

of robbery and similar crimes.[10] Finally there are offences for which the Ordinary may deprive the cleric of his office at his own discretion, for instance in the case of the illegal removal of secret documents from the archives of the diocesan curia.[11] These laws on privation *ipso jure* are important, for in our mind the Vicar-capitular remembering the principle *"Sede vacante nihil innovetur"*[12] should not ordinarily proceed to the removal of a diocesan consultor except on the grounds indicated or at least approaching them in weight. At first we were disposed to deny to the Vicar-general any power of removal over the diocesan consultors seeing that the Vicar-general cannot apparently name a substitute in such a case,[13] but closer study of canon 192 forces upon us the conclusion that even the Vicar-capitular possesses this power. In this canon we must first of all note that the word "privation" is used in a broader sense to include even removal outside of crime. Furthermore while the canon distinguishes only two kinds of offices viz: irremovable and removable, in our mind the removeable offices might be still further subdistinguished into those which are stated to be removable but without any qualification of the term and those that are removable *ad nutum.* To us it seems that there is a shade of difference between the two not enough perhaps to warrant dividing them into two separate species of offices but yet the *ad nutum* seems to signify a certain added ease of removal without even the necessity of a grave cause. If this explanation be admitted, we can note a certain difference between the tenure of the office of a Vicar-general for instance and that of the diocesan consultor. The signification of the expression *ad nutum* is well put by Father Augustine O. S. B.[14] who speaking of the office of the Vicar-general uses these words. "The removal of a vicar-general depends entirely on the good pleasure of

10 Can. 2354 p. 2.
11 Can. 2405.
12 Can. 436.
13 Can. 426 p. 5: Cf. also our remarks in Chap. IV.
14 Op. cit. II-396.

the bishop, who may take the office away, *with or without reason,*[15] and without any formality, summary or solemn procedure". These words are not to be taken to mean that the bishop should proceed in so temerarious a manner[16] but it shows how unhampered is the bishop when the office is *ad nutum* With the consultors on the other hand, to return to the subject matter of this work, the Bishop could not legally proceed in such a manner. We have called the diocesan consultors to be irremovable except for cause, and in this phrase we have only followed the example of our predecessors in this field. This is not to be confounded however with the irremovable offices mentioned in canon 192 p. 2. Theirs is only a relative irremovability and the term is justified only in contrast with offices which are *ad nutum.* When we have the prescriptions of canon 192 in mind i. e. when we wish to denote exactly the relation of the office of diocesan consultors to privation, then we must answer that they come rather within the removable offices for which paragraph 2 establishes the law. They are in other words removable indeed but only for cause and not *ad nutum.*

With these preliminary remarks by way of illumination we can now examine the dismissal of a diocesan consultor more closely in the light of the provisions of canon 192 p. 2. If a consultor is guilty of some offense for which as already mentioned there is established a punishment as privation *ipso jure* then, provided there is no scandal which would urge earlier action, it would be generally better perhaps to proceed against the cleric judicially as the privation under such circumstances would be nothing but a vindictive penalty and as such not to be applied except in a judicial fashion. But where scandal would intervene e. g. where the consultor would openly flout the superior or cause turbulence in the diocese[17] then as it is a removable office the Bishop

15 Italics are ours.
16 Blat, op. cit. II-337.
17 Cf. e. g. can. 2355.

need not await any judicial formality but immediately remove the unfaithful consultor with the advice however of other consultors in accordance with canon 428. The principle *"salus animarum suprema lex"*[18] finds its application here, and such a consultor need not cry for trial although recourse to the Holy See is always open.

Strict privation from office in the sense of a vindictive penalty will rarely be required. Our canon however under the same term treats of what may be termed simple removal i. e. the Ordinary may administratively decree for a just cause which may have no connection with guilt at all, that the consultor relinquish his office for the good of the diocese e. g. on account of the consultor's evident incapacity for the duties of the office. For such an administrative removal any just cause will suffice but a *just cause* is absolutely required. Decision as to what constitutes a just cause is left with the Ordinary but he must take counsel with his other consultors before he decides upon the dismissal of one of their number. Without a just cause the removal will indeed be valid in the sense that the injured occupant can only take recourse to the Holy See *in devolutivo* and not in *suspensivo*, but such a removal would be very quickly rescinded by the Holy See. Some of the causes for which a consultor could be justly removed are laid down in the old particular legislations. Thus the Third Plenary Council of Baltimore[19] mentions old age and infirmity and similar causes as the principal defects apt to render the consultor unfit for office. A grave dereliction is mentioned by the Council as another worthy cause of removal, but even a loss of reputation by the consultor entirely apart from his own guilt may be a sufficient reason for his dismissal. These words of Baltimore are repeated verbatim by the Councils of Sydney and Latin-America.[20]

We wish to point out in canon 192 the use of the word

18 Apud Augustine, op. cit. II-166.
19 N. 21.
20 Sydney, n. 34, Latin-America n. 1. 244.

"Ordinarius". As the Vicar-capitular is also an Ordinary we are constrained to admit that *per se* even the Vicar-capitular could remove a consultor from office. On the strength of this canon we would permit him to remove a consultor who for example suffered a very serious loss of reputation, but we think that as a rule the Vicar-capitular should not exercise this power as apparently he is unable to replace the consultor he would so deprive of office by naming a new member of the board, and as he is only a temporary administrator it would generally be better to leave all such questions affecting in some way the status of the diocese to the decision of the new bishop.

Influenced by this inability of the Vicar-capitular to appoint new consultors in the place of those he would depose Father Blat O. P.[21] doubts the power of the Vicar-capitular to remove a consultor if by that action he would lessen their number below the six or four required by canon 425 p. 1. There is something to this objection and it clearly indicates the inexpediency of the removal of a consultor by the Vicar-capitular but we are not quite prepared to deny this power to the Vicar-capitular in a particular instance even if it would lower their number below the minimum required by law. In our mind the absence of one consultor due to sickness would not invalidate the actions of the remaining members of the board provided all are legitimately convoked. In a similar fashion we fail to see why the absence of one member deprived justly of his office would invalidate the deliberations of those still in office. This however could be carried to extremes for in the abstract it would seem possible for the Vicar-capitular to remove gradually all consultors with the exception of the last one for whose removal he could not obtain the counsel of a remaining consultor as required by canon 428 and thus a dubious situation could be created with only one consultor. As a general rule therefore the Vicar-capitular should abstain

21 Op. cit. II-395.

from removing a diocesan consultor except where for some extraordinary reasons his removal should become urgent. In other cases let him urge upon the undesirable consultor, especially with the support of the other consultors, that he resign voluntarily and thus leave the Vicar-capitular free to appoint a new consultor. As most of the punitive purposes of privation can be equally well accomplished by suspension, which power the Vicar-capitular undeniably possesses, we think that the Vicar-capitular should ordinarily limit his punitive administration to this. This entire question however of the Vicar-capitular's right of removing a diocesan consultor from office is so involved in uncertainties that a clearing up of some of the doubts here indicated by responsible authorities would be welcome indeed. Before closing our remarks on this we may state that in case of a recourse to the Holy See against the action of the Ordinary in removing a consultor from office the competent congregation is that of the Sacred Council *(Sacra Congregatio Concilli)*. If however the consultor's removal has been decreed with the affirmative advice of the remaining consultors the dismissed consultor would best acquiesce to the decree of the Bishop as in such a supposition he may be presumed to have acted justly.

In this chapter we may briefly take up the question of the diocesan consultor's right to precedence. We have seen that the board of consultors has been established in imitation of and as temporary substitutes for the cathedral chapter. We have learned further that the New Code recognizes this institution and gives the board exactly the same powers as possessed by the cathedral chapter in so far as these powers have to do with the administration of the diocese. Would this recognition by the Code give to the diocesan consultors also the same precedure over the diocesan clergy as is enjoyed by the cathedral chapter?

In answer we can only state that this is matter ultimately to be settled by custom, although under the guidance of the respective Ordinaries. The New Code establishes only a few rules for precedence; they are principally contained in canon 106 where in paragraph 2 we are given the cardinal rule governing precedence viz: he who possesses authority over other persons has a right of precedence over these persons. This is the principle that must guide us in our own matter and since the diocesan consultors at least as a body possess some authority over the other diocesan clergy (which is more apparent when the see is vacant when they exercise real ordinary jurisdiction) they should be given precedence over all the other clergy with the sole exception of the Vicar-general. It is on this same principle that the cathedral chapter has been recognized as entitled to precedence over all the diocesan clergy.[22] As our diocesan consultors possess now all the rights and duties of the cathedral chapter in the administration of the diocese so it is only proper that they be also accorded the honorific rights of the cathedral chapter. Objection however can be made that the diocesan consultors are not actually a corporate body of the same nature as the cathedral chapter. To this we may answer that this may be the reason why the Code does not expressly mention diocesan consultors as possessing any rights of precedence but corporate union is not essentially necessary for precedence. Thus it is recognized that pastors enjoy precedence over those that are not pastors[23] and yet these pastors do not form a corporate body. Practically therefore we may answer in this fashion. As far as the common law is concerned the diocesan consultors have not a defined right to precedence; the matter is left to the respective Ordinaries[24] who however are obliged to establish such rules of precedence in their dioceses and to take into account the principles enunciated in canon 106. Where therefore the Bishop will execute the provisions of this canon there the diocesan consultors of necessity almost are to be assigned a position of precedence. This should especially

22 Can. 370; Wernz, op. cit. II-162.
23 Wernz, ibid.
24 Can. 106.

be done now that they are to all practical purposes the same as the cathedral chapter.

The only writer that has taken up the question of precedence with a view to conditions in the United States was Father Baart. In his *Legal Formulary*[25] he prefers to assign to diocesan consultors a position equal to that of the irremovable rectors so that the two would preceed *ex eaquo* the remaining clergy of the diocese excepting the Roman prelates. The reason given by Dr. Baart for such an arrangement was that the two classes together proposed the *terna* or the three names for the choice of a new bishop to the vacant see. As this privilege is now no longer possessed by either of these two groups it naturally cannot now be the ground upon which to settle their precedence. Furthermore to-day all our parishes are canonical parishes and their pastors real canonical parish-priests *(parochi)*. The irremovable pastors therefore possess to-day only a slight precedence over the other pastors while the diocesan consultors on the other hand have been now recognized by the universal law as taking in almost all respects the part of a cathedral chapter. In the light of these developments the order suggested by Rev. Dr. Peries, formerly Professor of Canon Law at the Catholic University in Washington[26] is to be preferred, viz: that the diocesan consultors take precedence over all the diocesan clergy.

Closely connected with the problem of their precedence is the question of what is the appropriate title to be given to diocesan consultors. The individual canons, members of the cathedral or collegiate chapter are by an universally recognized custom styled "Very Reverend." Can our diocesan consultors be so compared to the individual canons as to merit also the title of "Very Reverend"? Practice seems to be against any such interpretation. A casual comparison between the two would seem to lend weight to the propriety of giving the diocesan consultors this title of address but closer study reveals that the pre-

25 P. 136.
26 Apud Baart, op. cit. p. 137.

sent practice is perhaps better founded for the canons are appointed for life while the consultors hold their office for three years only. There would therefore be a certain incongruity in addressing a consultor as "Very Reverend" who some time later will have to be content with the simple title of "Reverend" when no longer a consultor. But the same objection would hold true against a Vicar-general and who most assuredly is to be called "Very Reverend", as he is for the time of his office entitled to all the prerogatives of honor given ordinarily to titular protonotaries apostolic.[27] The matter can not therefore be otherwise regulated than by custom but if the spirit of the new legislation be imitated and the diocesan consultors be compared as closely as possible with the cathedral chapter then too they are entitled to be called "Very Reverend" and the writer certainly would not condemn such a custom. Dr. Baart[28] indeed would term such a custom as preposterous although even before the New Code the opposite view was stoutly defended by a writer in the *American Ecclesiastical Review*[29] who mentions the Province of Milwaukee as having established in a provincial council the precedence of consultors which would also justify styling them "Very Reverend." In practice local usage will be the guide.

27 Cf. Augustine, op. cit. II-404.
28 Op. cit. p. 141, also p. 46.
29 Vol. XLIX-232.

CHAPTER VIII.

CHARACTER OF DUTIES IN GENERAL.

We come now to the discussion of the general character of the rights and duties of diocesan consultors. It is here that we find the greatest change in the status of diocesan consultors as compared with the former legislation and therefore it will necessitate treating the matter at some length. The particular rights and duties will be considered in subsequent chapters; here we shall strive to lay down the fundamental rules that must govern all the acts of the body of diocesan consultors.

Before considering the New Code on this point we must be permitted to recall briefly the historical course of this institution as already outlined at greater length in the first chapter of this work. We have seen that the institution of diocesan consultors was the result of efforts to obtain the purpose of the cathedral chapters in the common law of the universal church without some of their disadvantages that prevented their immediate erection in missionary countries. For this reason the rights and duties of diocesan consultors always resembled those of the cathedral chapter but not without considerable modification. The diocesan consultors, whereever established, were always considered to be like the cathedral chapter the official and legal council of the Bishop in matters pertaining to the government of the diocese, but in the application of this principle there were considerable divergences. For the cathedral chapters there was the quite definite legislation of the common law describing in what particular instances the advice or even the consent of the chapter was required. With the diocesan consultors the matter was left to local particular legislation.

The First Plenary Council of Baltimore[1] as it merely exhorted our bishops to constitute consultors in every diocese did not go beyond stating that their advice be asked whenever need should arise and lauded especially the custom already established in at least one diocese of having the consultors meet regularly every month for the discussion of diocesan affairs. The Second Plenary Council of Baltimore[2] did no more than reiterate in strong words the desirability of instituting consultors in every diocese. In the absence therefore of a more definite provision the bishop was neither absolutely required to institute consultors nor after their appointment was he strictly bound to take their council under pain of nullity. It is only the Third Plenary Council of Baltimore followed by the Plenary Councils of Sydney and Latin-America and the Provincial Council of Manila that made their institution obligatory and endowed them with definite rights and duties. By the acts of these councils the consultors were constituted the senate and the official advisers of the Bishop, much as the cathedral chapter and therefore in conformity with the general principles of law defining the relations between the Bishop and his council the former could not validly act without taking the advice of the latter where this was prescribed,[3] although having taken their advice he was not strictly obliged to follow it. This counsel was given by the diocesan consultors not individually but as an assembled body, by a majority vote, and if necessary they could resort to a secret vote.[4] The requirement of their consent was, as we have already noted, introduced only by the decree "*Maxima Cura*" of 1910 and that limited only to the selection of pro-synodal examiners or in filling a vacancy of either a synodal examiner or that of a parish-priest consultor.

Such then was the general character of the diocesan

1 n. VI, Lacensis III-146.
2 N. VI., Collection Lacensis III-146.
3 Smith, op. cit. I-499.
4 Acta et Decreta Conc. Balt. Plen. III, n. 21.

consultors' rights and duties before the promulgation of the New Code. The discipline was marked by an only imperfect definiteness; it was varied in the different regions where the diocesan consultors were found: they were therefore only a distant adumbration of the cathedral chapter of which they were temporarily to take place. Looked on under this aspect the change introduced by the New Code is almost revolutionary. There is no longer a list of certain acts for the valid execution of which the bishop requires the participation of diocesan consultors. The legislation is admirable for its simplicity. The Code breifly but cogently lays down the principle which makes the institution of diocesan consultors the same for all practical purposes as the cathedral chapter. Note the rights and duties of the cathedral chapter and you know immediately the rights and duties also of the diocesan consultors. This cardinal rule which we must always have in mind when treating of the rights and duties of diocesan consultors is to be found in canon 427 of the New Code which on account of its immense importance we shall be pardoned for quoting in its entirety. *"Coetus consultorum diocesanorum vices Capituli cathedralis, qua Episcopi senatus, supplet; quare quae canones ad gubernationem dioecesis, sive sede plena sive ea impedita aut vacante, Capitulo cathedrali tribuunt, ea de coetu quoque consultorum dioecesanorum intelligenda sunt."*

Before dissecting this all-important canon we must recall again the two fold nature of a cathedral chapter. All chapters, whether cathedral or collegiate, to use the very words of the New Code, are instituted for offering to God a more solemn worship in churches.[5] With this generic duty of the chapters the diocesan consultors have nothing expressly in common. But the cathedral chapter as distinguished from the collegiate chapter has another duty which practically is the chief reason for its existence. This is, to continue in the words of the same

5 Can. 391.

canon, that it assist the bishop in the manner prescribed by law as his senate and council and to supply his place by governing the diocese during the vacancy of the episcopal see. It is therefore in its nature as the official and legal advising body that the diocesan consultors supply the place of a cathedral chapter. And that there may be no possible doubt canon 427 continues to state most explicitly that any right or duty assigned by law to the cathedral chapter in matters pertaining to the administration of the diocese, whether the see be occupied or vacant, or the administration of the see only impeded, is to be applied with equal force and value to the body of diocesan consultors. How admirable indeed is this plan. In these few words the New Code has brought about an orderly uniformity in all bishops' councils in the Latin rite, for in all dioceses of the Western Church we must find either the cathedral chapter or its substitute the diocesan consultors, and both of these hereafter will perform the same fundamental duties and enjoy the same basic rights in every part of the world. Canons like this one give us an insight into the true character of the New Code, among the purposes of which was precisely the restoration of this fundamental unity of discipline in the Church wherever practicable.

We have discussed before the possible meanings of the words *"coetus consultorum."* (Chap. II.) Here it will suffice to recall that by these words the body of the diocesan consultors is placed on a par with the cathedral chapter as a whole, and not individual consultors with the individual members of the cathedral chapter or the canons. The schema of the New Code used somewhat different words in this canon. It proposed that the Ordinaries require the counsel or consent of consultors in the manner established in a preceding canon (what now is canon 106) in every affair in which the canons oblige the bishop to take counsel or seek consent of his cathedral chapter. The wording of the schema omitted therefore the power to elect an administrator during the vacancy of the see but this was provided for in another canon where rules were laid down for the election of a Vicar-capitular. In accordance therefore with this canon 427 whenever we come across the word *capitulum* in the Code and the context shows that reference is made to a cathedral chapter *ut Episcopi senatus,* the provisions laid down there are to be applied with equal force to the body of diocesan consultors unless it is clear that the canon happens to be concerned only with the internal regime of the chapter. For the same reason such canons as 1182, 712 do not apply to the diocesan consultors because they clearly refer to the cathedral church as the church of the chapter considered in its generic aspect only viz: as a college of clerics exercising or performing more solemn worship. Nor do we qualify the word chapter by the adjective "cathedral" because there are a few places in the Code where the word is used without the adjective and yet the context clearly shows that the cathedral chapter is meant. As a rule therefore whenever the word *capitulum* occurs in the Code, outside of chapter V in Tit. VII Lib. II which applies to chapters only, the prescriptions therein contained will apply generally to diocesan consultors likewise. The presumption is against the contrary likelihood.

In reference to the canons which concern the internal government of the chapter (as in the aforementioned chap. V etc.) we must understand that due to its twofold character of duties the cathedral chapter possesses also a twofold organization. As constituting the *ex officio* senate and council of the bishop, in which it is imitated by the diocesan consultors, it has the Bishop as its head and noblest member.[6] But apart from this, in common with all other chapters it has its own distinct organization as a college of clerics organized for greater solemnity of worship and then it possesses rights and duties entirely its own so that the Bishop in this aspect of the chapter is neither its head nor even a member of it. It is this phase of their organization that is considered

6 Cf. Smith in the American Catholic Quarterly Review, Oct. 1878, p. 711.

chiefly in the cited chap. V etc. and hence there is nothing in that entire section which would concern the body of diocesan consultors except in so far as it may offer guidance in some of the analogous duties of the diocesan consultors.

Before taking up the rights and duties in particular let us first obtain a proper notion of what the law means when it requires consent or counsel of the diocesan consultors, for questions of counsel and consent almost exhaust the duties of the diocesan consultors. This matter is regulated for all similar cases in canon 105.[7] According to this canon whenever the consent of the consultors is required the Bishop or the Vicar-capitular, would act invalidly if they should proceed contrary to the vote of the majority of their council, in other words their acts in such a case would be altogether null and void. If however it is counsel only that is required by the law, then for valid action the Bishop, or the Vicar-capitular, must hear and take their counsel but is obliged to do no more, i. e. he can legally act contrary even to the unanimous advice of his consultors although of course the law urges him not to do so without a sufficiently grave reason. It is somewhat important to note the strict necessity for consulting the persons prescribed by law, for since the canon uses the words *"satis est"* one might at first impression be inclined to interpret them in the sense that it is sufficient for the bishop to take the consultors' counsel without however being obliged to take it *ad validitatem.* On the contrary therefore the word is simply used to determine the limit of the requirement but there is a most positive necessity of taking the advice

7 "Cum ius statuit Superiorem ad agendum indigere consensu vel consilio aliquarum personarum:

"Si consensus exigatur, Superior contra earundem votum invalide agit; si consilium tantum, per verba, ex. gr.: de consilio consultorum, vel audito Capitulo, parocho, etc., satis est ad valide agendum ut Superior illas personas audiat; quam vis autem nulla obligatione teneatur ad eorum votum, etsi concors, accendendi, multum tamen, si plures audiendae sint personae concordibus earundem suffragiis deferat, nec ab eisdem, sine praevalenti ratione, suo iudicio aestimanda, discedat;......"

when prescribed, under pain of nullity, for such was always the principle of law in cases where counsel is prescribed and this canon is to be interpreted in no other manner.[8] What the canon wishes to establish is that having heard the consultors' advice the bishop has no strict obligation to follow their counsel even it is should be unanimous. It is only the dictate of common sense however that, as subsequently laid down ordinarily the bishop should not presumptuously disregard their advice but esteem it much especially when many persons have been heard (which should be true of consultors who at the very least will number four) and their advice is more or less concordant; so that the bishop should seriously weigh the matter in his conscience before for a reason he would deem sufficient he should decide to act contrary to the counsel given.

Of no less importance is the next paragraph of the canon establishing the manner of obtaining this advice or consent.[9] Whenever more than two persons are concerned, as is precisely the case with diocesan consultors, their advice or consent cannot be obtained individually but they must be legitimately convoked unless they all happen to be already present.[10] Analogically the remaining provisions of canon 192 which strictly has to do with elections is to be applied to convocations in general, so that if any one be passed over in the convocation the action of the assembly transacted without his presence is to be considered either null or at least rescindible by the proper superior as the case may be.[11] It would be well in convoking extraordinary meetings to mention in the call the purpose of the assembly so far as this would be feasible.

8 Alexander III (c. 4, 5, De his, quae fiunt....III,10) apud Smith op. sit. p. 499. Cf. also Ferreres, op. cit. I n. 229.

9 20. "Si requiratur consensus vel consilium non unius tantum vel alterius personae, sed plurium simul, eae personae legitime convocentur, salvo praescripto can. 162, p. 4, et mentem suam manifestent: Superior autem pro sua prudentia ac negotiorum gravitate potest eas adigere ad iusiurandum de secreto servando praestandum."

10. Can. 162, p. 4.

11 Ferreres, op. cit. I, n. 230; Augustine, op. cit. II-448.

The accidental presence however of which canon 162 speaks must take on the nature of a recognized assembly, otherwise it ceases to answer the purpose. If therefore the consultors should all happen to be present with the Bishop at some festive occasion, he could not take their advice in public before all the other clergy which would perhaps interfere with the consultors' freedom of expressing their true opinion.[12] When properly assembled the consultors are to openly manifest their mind and as they have been honored with the appointment to the position of being the Bishop's legal advisers, they are obliged to perform the service required with the proper reverence and express their opinion faithfully and sincerely.[13] The bishop should he consider it advisable by reason of the gravity of the business discussed, may even require the consultors to emit an oath for preserving secrecy. As Father Ferreres S. J.[14] remarks, this is a *"Secretum commissum"* and therefore would oblige by the virtue of justice.

This canon has another great importance to one who would prefer to hold that the body of diocesan consultors is not a moral person. If the consultors are not a collegiate body there would be an apparent lack of legislation for the conduct of the diocesan consultors' office. This lacuna in that supposition would for the greater part be supplied by the provisions of this canon 105. Whether they are a moral person or not it is clear that they must be legitimately convoked and manifest their opinion as an assembled body, not as individuals.

For the rest our cue is to be taken from the analogy with cathedral chapters from the former particular legislation and from custom. Thus it would perhaps be commendable to approach the spirit of canon 397 and have the diocesan consultors assist the Bishop likewise in his pontifical, liturgical functions and especially the last number of the same canon prescribing that the various

12 Augustine, op. cit. II-36.

13 Can. 105 n. 30. "Omnes de consensu vel consilio requisiti debent ea qua par est reverentia, fide ac sinceritate sententiam suam aperire."

14 Op. cit. I, n. 230.

members of the body have a right to convoke and preside at the meetings in the order of their precedence. This last would have its importance during the vacancy of the see when question might arise as to who is to convoke the body of consultors for the election of the administrator. While the diocesan consultors, not being a permanent body, could not perhaps very well have some permanent statutes yet the spirit of can. 410n. 1 could laudably be imitated by having the consultors determine upon their entrance upon the duties of the office a certain definie mode of procedure, a few regulations that would guide them in their future deliberations whenever assembled either in conformity with a statute requiring their regular monthly meeting or in answer to a specific call from the Bishop.

The New Code omits to prescribe any definite frequency or regularity to the meetings of diocesan consultors. The schema indeed proposed in one of its canons that the diocesan consultors should be convoked by their Bishop at least four times a year at regularly established intervals or, if that be impossible, they should meet at least twice a year apart from the extraordinary meetings necessitated by any business that may occur requiring their counsel or consent. This proposal was practically a repetition of what is required by the Third Plenary Council of Baltimore.[15] Why the Code did not retain the proposal of the schema is not within our ability to answer. Perhaps the Code desired to leave some flexibility in the matter and allow it to be ruled rather by local legislation or custom. But in the absence of a definite regulation by the Code there is all the more justification for establishing say by diocesan statute the time of regular meetings which would suffice for the convocation of diocesan consultors. Certainly the practice of almost never convoking the diocesan consultors does not at all answer the spirit of this legislation. The mind of the Church in this regard is probably best shown by the re-

15 N. 21.

gulations approved for English chapters which are required to meet regularly once a month.[16] Such is already the custom in many of the better organized dioceses of this country and it would be commendable if it were universally established by diocesan statutes, as was done by Bishop Portier in the first synod of Mobile,[17] that this council meet at a regular day and hour each month for the discussion of the general affairs of the diocese. In the absence of such a diocesan provision or at least custom there remains for the dioceses of the United States the legislation of the Third Plenary Council of Baltimore[18] which not being contrary to the law of the Code but only *praeter Codicem*[19] still obtains in full force i. e. the bishops of United States are still obliged in virtue of this conciliar law to convoke the diocesan consultors four times a year at stated intervals and only where this is impossible can he limit the number of convocations to two a year. But this refers only to regular meetings; extraordinary meetings can be called whenever an affair requiring the diocesan consultors' advice or consent should arise. By analogy with cathedral chapters[20] the regular meeting established by statute or definite custom needs not a special convocation but to assemble the consultors at other times the Bishop must issue a formal call.

Can any one other than the Bishop assemble the consultors? The cathedral chapter has its own independent existence distinct from its quality as the senate of the Bishop and therefore may be convoked not only by the Bishop but also by its own head (generally called the provost) or even whenever a majority of the canons may deem it opportune. Here the analogy between the chapter and the body of diocesan consultors fails somewhat, because the duties of the latter are confined to their character as the Bishop's senate and hence they have no in-

16 Collectio Lacensis III-923 n. 8.
17 a. 1835.
18 N. 21.
19 Can. 6, 22.
20 Can. 411.

dependent head apart from the Bishop. They can therefore ordinarily be convoked only by the Bishop or by him who takes the place during the vacancy of the see i. e. by the Administrator or the Vicar-capitular. They could never hold independent meetings (and this we admit would constitute an objection against the opinion that the body of diocesan consultors is a moral person) except on two occasions, when the see is vacant or when the administration by the Bishop or his delegate is impeded and then their independent administration is limited to eight days during which time they must elect a Vicar-capitular to whom then the ordinary jurisdiction of the diocese passes. During such an *interregnum* it would fall upon the senior member of the board of consultors to convoke them and this seniority would be regulated by canon 106. Therefore even if there should be an auxiliary bishop in the diocese and he be not a member of the body of diocesan consultors, he would have no power to convoke the consultors. If he be one of the consultors (and such, we think, will usually be the case) it will devolve upon him to assemble the gathering. If all are priests only and one of them be a domestic prelate or even any other honorary member of the Roman Court we think perhaps he would have the right to summon the body to a meeting. For the rest the precedence is settled by seniority of ordination or finally by age. After the first meeting the subsequent gatherings could very well be regulated by the majority vote of the entire body.

This leads us to consider what is to be regarded as the act of the body of diocesan consultors as a whole. We prefer to regard the board of consultors as a moral person and therefore apply without any difficulty canon 101 regulating the acts of such collegiate moral persons. But even if the opposite be held this canon must be applied by analogy on the general principle "*Ubi eadem juris ratio eadem debet esse juris dispositio*" and in accordance with canon 20 of the New Code. In the aforementioned canon it is laid down as a general principle (i. e.

in the absence of a contrary particular legislation) that whatever has obtained the approval of the absolute majority of those present and voting, laying aside of course the votes that are null, that is to be regarded as the act of the body as a whole. Once therefore a legitimate convocation has been made it is immaterial how many of the members are present as there is no mention anywhere of a certain quorum being required.[21] In our mind however it would perhaps be wiser to postpone a meeting if less than one-half of the members should be present. Father Augustine O. S. B.[22] would require at least three to be present on the principle "Tres faciunt collegium." This is a point that could best be settled by a diocesan statute or at least by a previous agreement of the consultors, say on the occasion of their first meeting. In any vote therefore, whether it concerns the election of a Vicar-capitular (Administrator) or the offering of counsel and especially consent, the majority vote of those present decides. But if two votes be taken in a certain matter and the result is that neither proposition obtains an absolute majority then in the third vote the relative majority or as we call it in the United States the plurality of votes decides. If even this be lacking then we confess we face an apparently insoluble difficulty. Ordinarily the presiding officer would cast the deciding vote but the diocesan consultor have no independent president. A certain precedence can be given to the senior member but in the supposition he will have already cast his vote. The question might have considerable importance when an act requiring the consent of consultors would come up. In a diocese having six consultors where the vote for giving such consent would continue to stand three and three who will decide the tie? With some timidity, and always *salvo meliori judicio*, we venture to suggest that perhaps then the bishop could proceed validly on his judgment for he is in a way the

21 Fr. Augustine op. cit. II-25 cities Bouix, De Capitulis, p. 182 as requiring a presence of two thirds for a quorum.
22 Op. cit. II-448.

head of this body of diocesan consultors and then too it could not be said that he would act against the will of the majority. In the election of a Vicar-capitular (Administrator) there is a simpler solution for the one senior by ordination or at least in age is held to be elected after the third vote.

The New Code does not seem to require secret balloting except for elections[23] hence as a general principle the voting may be open and public. But for us the Third Plenary Council of Baltimore is establishing that the advice of consultors be given *"collegialiter"* expressly states that whenever the consultors should so desire they may give it by secret vote.[24] While the other councils omit mention of this it follows from the very nature of such bodies that they may decide at any time by a majority in open vote to resort to secret balloting for decision of a given question.

It is indeed nowhere laid down that one of the board of consultors should be made a secretary, but such is the practice obtaining in several of the dioceses of the United States and we think the idea should be encouraged. The recording of the minutes of any assembly adds to its orderly procedure and in questions of consent it would provide a proper record of the action taken. Where there is a secretary on the board of diocesan consultors in the United States he is generally the bishop's chancellor to which there can be scarcely any objection. Father Nilles S. J. who wrote a commentary upon the Third Plenary Council of Baltimore insists that it is of obligation that the minutes of their meetings and acts be kept recorded in writing.[25] Closely conneced with this is the recommendation that the Bishop executing those acts which require the consent or counsel of consultors should expressly mention in the documents narrating or decreeing the act that the prescribed consent or counsel

23 Can. 169 p. 1, n. 2.
24 N. 21.
25 P. 67.

has been obtained.[26] This is often done in the Papal constitutions although the Pope is not obliged to take any advice. A rule that may also be well observed by diocesan consultors as the same reason for both, is that of canon 418 p. 2 forbidding more than one third of the chapter to be absent at one and the same time. As sometimes occasion may arise suddenly necessitating the convocation of the consultors the purpose of their institution would not be met with if too many should happen to be absent.

We can now take up the rights and duties of the diocesan consultors in particular. For convenience of consideration we shall divide these into those obtaining *Sede Plena* or *Sede Impedita* or finally *Sede Vacante.* We shall first take up the common law of the Church and then any particular legislation that may obtain in addition to the Code. For the rest custom, or diocesan statutes or perhaps new plenary or provincial councils or even special prescriptions of the Holy See, may at times add to their duties. An example of this last may be had in the decree of the Sacred Consistorial Congregation of July 1916 addressed to the Bishops of Canada concerning clerical dress in which the Bishops were instructed that they may alter the custom regulating clerical vesture on consultation with the chapter or their diocesan consultors. The Bishop therefore should not consider the points laid down in the general law as requiring the counsel or consent of his consultors to be the miximum expected of him but rather as the minimum. Let it be the rule rather that in all important decisions the advice of consultors be taken and so far as feasible accepted. For our guide in the following chapters we shall first take the former particular legislation, particularly that of Baltimore as the most extensive. We shall thus be better able to show where and what changes have been introduced by the New Code in this matter.

26 Ibidem.

CHAPTER IX.

RIGHTS AND DUTIES *SEDE PLENA*.

As used in this chapter the expression *"sede plena"* is to be understood in a somewhat stricter sense than the one in which it is ordinarily used. As here treated it is in contradistinction not only to *"sede vacante"* but also to *"sede impedita."* It means therefore not only that the see must be occupied and filled by its own proper bishop-Ordinary but also that he be in no way prevented from the exercise of his jurisdiction e. g. by captivity. The see is considered to be occupied from the moment the new bishop has presented his letters of appointment to the board of diocesan consultors where they are found either personally or through a procurator. The see ceases to be occupied when the bishop dies or is transferred or deprived of his office or he himself presents his resignation. In the case of the last three however the see does not become vacant until the action of the Holy See is signified to the occupant.[1]

ARTICLE I.

Their relation to the Diocesan Synod.

The first attribute assigned to the diocesan consultors by the Third Baltimore Plenary Council was that their advice be asked in convoking and promulgating the diocesan synod.[2] The First Plenary Council of Sydney established almost the same viz: their advice in assigning the time for the annual synod and their opinion as to the proposal of new statutes in the synod.[3] The Latin-

1 Can. 430 p. 1, 190.
2 N. 20, 10.
3 N. 31-(3)-a, b.

American Council required their advice only for the convocation of the synod[4] although among the *postulata* of that council was the request that the bishops of those countries be permitted to convoke to their synods only one-half of the pastors or only a certain number for which they were to obtain the advice of their consultors. We do not know whether this *postulatum* was granted or conceded in the form it was asked.

What does the New Code establish in this regard? There appear to be some modifications introduced in the former legislation concerning diocesan synods. Before the New Code under the old common law the Bishop required no one's consent to convoke the synod, on the contrary he was obliged to assemble it annually. In reference however to the synodal statutes while the Bishop was recognized to be the sole legislator yet he was required to present to his cathedral chapter the plan of his proposed new ordinances a reasonable time before the synod and to ask its advice thereon.[5] The Code on the contrary omits any mention of such a requirement and therefore it must be regarded as abrogated.[6] Instead the Bishop is now required to submit in advance the proposed new ordinances to all those that have been summoned to the synod[7] and to permit free discussion of all these proposals in preparatory gatherings held under his own presidency or of another acting in his name.[8] These preparatory sessions were known even before[9] but to-day they are of strict obligation. The purpose therefore of the chapter's previous counsel will now be even better attained by hearing the opinions not only of the few members of the chapter or the board of diocesan consultors but of the major part perhaps of the clergy of the diocese and hence it is no longer necessary to obtain the advice of the chapter or the consultors' alone.

4 N. 245, 10.
5 Wernz, op. cit. II-n. 863.
6 Can. 6 n. 6.
7 Can. 360 p. 2.
8 Can. 361.
9 Wernz, 1. c.

But what of our own particular legislation ? The decree of the Baltimore Council on this subjct was interpreted by Dr. S. B. Smith[10] and Father Fanning S. J.[11] to mean not that the bishop was obliged to obtain the consultors' advice on the convocation of the synod but rather as stated above with regard to the chapters, he was required to lay before the consultors the decrees and regulations he intended to promulgate at the synod and thus to obtain their opinion and advice on the proposed statutes.

What is to be done now after the promulgation of the Code in this welter of overlapping if not conflicting legislation. For the solution of the difficulty we must always have before us the general principle that posterior laws must be so far as possible reconciled with the preceding legislation[12] and only when the conflict is clear and evident is the old to be considered abrogated[13] especially when an universal law seems to overlap an old particular law. But the legislation of the Third Plenary Council of Baltimore, and of the Sydney and Latin-American Councils cannot be said to be opposed to the new general legislation and hence their rules in this regard must be considered to be still in full force. There is no serious objection to retaining the necessity of obtaining the consultors' advice as to the time of convoking the diocesan synod but in view of the now obligatory preparatory sessions the advice of the diocesan consultors on the proposed statutes themselves is now not so important but until a new Plenary Council ordains otherwise the old procedure must still be observed.[14]

We might as well point here an innovation not men-

10 Op. cit. p. 499 ff.

11 Cath. Enc., XIV-388, article "Synod."

12 Can. 23.

13 Can. 6 n. 1.

14 In passing we might note that this is but one point indicating the advisability of holding a new Plenary Council at an early date in all the countries affected and particularly in the United States to revise the legislation of the former councils and to bring the discipline into greater conformity with that prescribed by the New Code.

tioned formerly in the same specific manner and that is the requirement of Canon 358 p. 1 n. 2. that the diocesan consultors are to be called *ex officio* to attend the diocesan synod and that they are bound by law to obey this call. As all having the care of souls were summoned to attend the diocesan synods in the United States this new provision will not effect any material change here since generally diocesan consultors are chosen from among pastors. But if it should happen that a diocesan consultor be chosen say from among the professors of the seminary, by the provisions of this canon he is to be called to attend the synod in virtue of his office as diocesan consultor. It has also its application if the consultor should live outside the episcopal city for the New Code requires only the pastors of the city in which the synod is convoked to attend.[15]

By way of a brief summary the following procedure may be suggested in agreement with both the New Code and the former particular legislation. When the decennial period of canon 356 is approaching its end, or the Bishop for other reasons should think that time has arrived for another diocesan synod, let him consult his board of diocesan consultors as to the proper time (and place) of holding the synod. This settled he may well discuss with them in advance some of the possible *agenda* at this synod and appoint one or more commissions of the clergy of the diocese to suggest other business of the synod and in a general way prepare all for the proper celebration of the synod. The final draft of ordinances prepared by these commissions might be again discussed by the Bishop in common with his consultors and then a copy of this schema must be presented to each one of the clergy who is to attend the synod and opportunity must be given to them all to make their suggestions in preliminary or so-called preparatory sessions of the synod. Before finally promulgating the new ordinances in the solemn session of the diocesan synod the Bishop must

15 Can. 358 p. 1 n. 6.

by Baltimore and Sydney law submit the draft settled upon for the consultors' advice and opinion. Membership of diocesan consultors on the preliminary commissions or their presence at the preparatory sessions would not satisfy Baltimore or Sydney law in its completeness because their presence at those sessions would not be *ex officio* or rather to satisfy Baltimore and Sydney law their action must be taken *collegialiter* and hence apart from the other clergy.

ARTICLE II.

Their connection with the union, transfer, division, dismembration or suppression of parishes (benefices).

The second case in which the Third Plenary Council of Baltimore required the advice of consultors was in reference to the dismemberment of missions or parishes.[16] The same necessity of their advice was prescribed by the Sydney[17] and the Latin-American[18] councils but this last added also the union of parishes. Both these provisions are retained in the New Code but in somewhat different terms and the requirement of the consultors' advice is extended also to the suppression of parishes (benefices).

The Baltimore council in its decree on this point used the word *"missio"* or *"parochia"* to include all the congregations or missions or as they were formerly wont to be called "quasi-parishes" in the United States for real canonical parishes were held to be practically nonexistent in the United States before the Code.[19] In the common law for the dismemberment or division of a canonical parish the consent of the cathedral chapter was required.[20] For missions generally the advice of the

16 N. 20-20.
17 N. 31-(3-c.)
18 N. 245-20.
19 Cath. Enç. XI-501.
20 Smith, op. cit. 502.

Bishop's or the Superior's (Vicar-Apostolic or Prefect-Apostolic) council was required.[21]

Dismembration and division are not really synonymous terms.

Dismemberment strictly speaking, means the taking away of a portion of a territory of one parish and assigning it to another be that second parish new or old. Division on the other hand refers only to the formation of new parishes and the territory of the new parish is not taken from several old parishes but one territory of an old parish is divided into two parts, one remaining the old parish and the other becoming the new. As far as the canonical procedure is concerned the norms to be observed in either of these two cases are identical, it being therefore only a question of terminology.[22]

Passing by the old legislation let us see what the New Code lays down in this important regard. In the first place let it be noted that it is now almost absolutely certain that all parishes and hence even the parishes in the United States, or other countries in similar circumstances, are really and truly benefices. This statement may surprise many yet only in such a way will the canons of the Code in this regard be properly understood. The New Code accepts parishes as merely one of the most important species of the genus benefice and for this reason much of the legislation laid down for parishes is indiscriminately intermingled with that on benefices. Since the Code does not visualize a parish which at least generally will not be a benefice *ipso facto* it does not repeat specifically for parishes what it has already laid down for benefices in general, except in so far as the special character of parishes would require a certain modification of the law on benefices in general. Whatever therefore is common to all benefices including parishes is not treated under the latter heading but under the former. Hence for the most part one will look in vain in the index of the Code for such subjects as the

21 Zitelli, op. cit. 188.
22 Can. 1421.

union, suppression, division or dismembration of parishes, because all these points are treated under the title on benefices. There is indeed in the Code a special reference to the division and dismembration of parishes due to the specific character of a parochial benefice but even this presupposes that the fundamental canons on the division or dismemberment of benefices have been taken account of.

As those who have written on the New Code in the United States hitherto have either ignored or positively denied the existence of benefices in this country a brief explanation of this point is in order, leaving to others the treatment of this point *ex professo*. Owing to the requirements necessary to constitute a canonical parish in the old legislation it was generally recognized that with the possible exception of a few parishes in San Francisco and one in New Orleans there were no canonical parishes and a *fortiori* no parochial benefices in this country.[23] With the promulgation of the Code however the definition of a parish was somewhat modified and principally in this that now it is certainly sufficient that the pastor be stable, permanent but not necessarily perpetual i. e. appointed *ad vitam.*[24] For this and other reasons which we need not mention here it was the almost unanimous opinion of canonists immediatly after the appearance of the New Code that our parishes are canonical parishes. This was subsequently confirmed by Roman documents.[25] But strangely enough the same commentators that fought so strenuously for the canonical character of the parishes in the United States did not seem to advert that the very same arguments advanced by them to prove that they are canonical parishes prove them almost *ipso facto* to be benefices for the elements of the two questions are almost exactly identical. In particular the new definition of the endowment *(dos)* of a

23 Cf. e. g. Wernz, op. cit. II-n. 822, not. 25 in fine: Augustine, op. cit. II-523.
24 Can. 454.
25 S. C. Consist., decl. 1 aug. 1919.

benefice in canon 1410 should be noted, to constitute which the voluntary offerings of the faithful are now sufficient especially where coupled with the stole fees. The only argument of any weight that could be advanced against the contention that our parishes are benefices is that a formal decree of erection of a parish as a benefice is required. But the Holy See has recognized as sufficient the old decree of erecting our so-called quasi-parishes to constitute them to-day real parishes with the changed definition of a parish in the New Code so it must be held that that same decree will now be sufficient to constitute our parishes benefices with the changed notion of both the benefice itself and the endowment *(dos)* in the New Code. For the rest, we may only mention that this contention possesses the highest possible extrinsic authority, being held by most prominent canonists not only in this country but also at Rome by persons quite conversant with the circumstances of the question. It would require therefore only a presentation through the proper channels of the question to the Commission for the interpretation of the New Code to obtain a formal authentic pronouncement of this nature. If however one should in the meantime be unwilling to accept the contention here advanced or in the improbable event of a contrary decision from Rome then we must turn again to canon 20 and on the principles of analogy apply the canons on the union, division etc. of benefices to our parishes also.

With these preliminary remarks we can now understand the provisions of the new legislation in this regard. The New Code abrogates the former requirement of the consent of the chapter and changes it to mere counsel, *"audito Capitulo"*.[26] This of course means that where there are diocesan consultors their advice must be taken in addition to that of the rectors concerned and this for the validity of the decree. But, and this must be stressed, the new legislation is much more extensive

26 Can. 1428.

for it includes not only dismemberment and division of parishes (and other benefices) but also the union, suppression and transfer of parishes (benefices). Of the former conciliar legislation only the Latin-American Council[27] considered union of parishes in addition to their division.

Division and dismemberment we have already defined. Union is defined for us authentically by the very legislator in canon 1419. It is suppressive *(exstinctiva)* when the title of two or more parishes (benefices) is suppressed and instead one new parish is erected, or one parish (benefice) is so united to another that only the latter continues to exist. An union known technically as *"aeque principalis"* is had when the parishes (benefices) remain as they were nor is one subjected to another so that there is no change in the status of the parish so united except that they are henceforth governed always by one pastor. In reference to this kind of union it must be noted that to constitute such an union it is not sufficient to have one pastor administer several congregations for a time only, but it must be in a certain manner permanent so that they are conferred in one title not only to one man but in a similar manner to his successors. No counsel of the consultors is therefore strictly necessary if the bishop, say for a lack of priests, would for a time entrust the *administration* of one parish to a pastor of another but who obtains no title in the second parish. Finally there is the union *"minus principalis"* also called union by accession or subjection in which the benefices (parishes) remain indeed but one or more are subjected to another as an accessory to the principal. In the union therefore *"aeque principalis"* the accounts of each church would be kept separately; in the *"minus principalis"* the revenues would all be transferred to the principal church. The different species may now have a very practical application in this country. With the changing character of the population in some of the larger cities of the

27 N. 245-20.

United States it not unfrequently happens that parishes that were once so important and successful as to be raised to the status of irremovable rectorships are later overwhelmed by a non-catholic population and in the original territory of the parish scarcely a handful of parishioners will be found, unable of course to support the immense parish plant. In such a case one of the above species of union should be resorted to with the advice of the diocesan consultors. A transfer of a benefice and specifically a parish would rarely occur in this country in the present circumstances. It seems possible only where there would be several churches (e. g. a shrine) within the territorial limits of the parish and the title of the parochial church would be transferred from the old church to one of these formerly non-parochial churches. We may also mention transfer or even the entire suppression of a parish can be resorted to by the proper authorities as a species of vindictive penalty upon not only the clergy but also the laity.[28] For this case there is the specific provision of canon 2292 that the Ordinary could only decree such a penal transfer or suppression of a parish with the advice of the chapter or in our case the diocesan consultors.

In all the aforementioned cases therefore the Ordinary before he can validly proceed must not only hear the pastors interested but also on our case consult the diocesan consultors. These last in offering their advice should remember that all the aforementioned acts are considered odious in law and therefore require a cause of proportionate gravity. For the good of the souls however a greater freedom is allowed in the matter of the division or dismemberment of parishes,[29] but even in that case if a so-called vicariate perpetual is possible this is to be preferred to the erection of a new parish. Perpetual vicariates are perhaps unknown in this country but in the mind of the writer they would perhaps offer a solution for the difficulty in establishing new national pa-

28 Can. 2291 n. 30.
29 Can. 1427.

rishes for which an apostolic indult is necessary.[30] Our outlying missions would not differ very much from the notion of perpetual vicariates except that these last have a resident priest although only a vicar and subject to the real pastor.

The causes required for union or transfer of benefices need not detain us here but will be found in the Code in Lib. III, tit. XXV, cap. II. We need only mention that such a decree must be in writing[31] and that a canonical cause is so required for all these actions that without it the action is altogether invalid, although recourse to the Holy See is granted only *in devolutivo*. Therefore there must be an investigation of the causes advanced by the Bishop for his intended action. It may also be noted that the total suppression of a benefice (including parishes) in such a manner that no new parish (benefice) is erected in its stead is reserved to the Holy See.[32] This illustrates what permanency is desired for all benefices and therefore even our parishes. Only in exraordinary circumstances would such a suppression of a parochial benefice be granted but the writer can scarcely conceive where this would occur with relation to a parish. The Ordinary can with the advice of his diocesan consultors suppress a parish as a vindictive penalty[33] therefore Canon 1422 must rather have in mind suppression of a parish without even assigning the territory to another parish or more correctly it considers only a case where the Ordinary would intend to destroy the benefice by removing all of its goods or endowment.

To summarize then either because our parishes are benefices, or at least by analogy in view of canon 20, the advice of diocesan consultors is now required not only in the division of parishes but also in the different species of their union, as well as in the case of their dismemberment, transfer or penal suppression. Certain

30 Can. 216 p. 4.
31 Can. 1428.
32 Can. 1422.
33 Can. 2291 n. 30, 2292.

species of union to be considered in the following article require their own norms to the discussion of which we shall now proceed.

ARTICLE III.

Their function in reference to the union or the entrusting of a parish to a religious community.

The third case requiring diocesan consultors' advice in Baltimore law was the question of offering a parish or mission to a religious order or institute for administration, in which case also the permission of the Holy See was required.[34] Similar legislation was passed in the Sydney[35] and Latin-American[36] councils. The New Code expresses the entire question in considerably different words. Strictly speaking the pastor of a canonical parish, as ours are now also, must be a person either physical or at least moral i. e. legal. But when a parish is given to a moral person as a pastor the process is no other than one of union of two moral persons for the parish is certainly a non-collegiate moral person.[37] This union is regulated by the provisions of canon 1423 with which are closely connected canons 1425 and 452. In the former common law to give the administration of a parish to the religious required the consent of the chapter.[38] The reason for such stringent formalities was that such an act was regarded as a species of perpetual alienation of ecclesiastical property which process the Church has for a long time surrounded with certain safeguards.

What has been said about parishes being benefices in the preceding article applies with equal force here. While our missions before the promulgation of the New Code were not canonical parishes, still less benefices the

34 N. 20-30.
35 N. 31-3-d.
36 N. 245-3.
37 Can. 99.
38 Smith, op. cit., 504.

law of Baltimore will be better understood when we know the principle that regulated this question in common law which principle remains in equal force to-day. It is that secular benefices (parishes) are to be conferred upon secular priests; regular (or now more correctly religious) benefices must be given to regulars (religious).[39] This ancient principle is now embodied in the the New Code in canon 1442.

With this as an axiom one will readily recognize that to go contrary to this rule permission of the Holy See would be required, especially since in regard to parishes there is a certain unfitness that they be administered generally by the religious who by the nature of their state of life are not intended to mingle with seculars as much as is required for the proper exercise of parochial duties. Hence it is that the Holy See prefers to reserve the decision as to the expediency of entrusting a particular parish to the religious to its own judgment.

The legislation of the New Code in this entire matter is much more extensive than either of the three Plenary Councils has considered. In the first place as regards parishes we have the express prohibition of canon 452 p. 1 invalidating any union of a parish *pleno jure* with a moral person so that this moral person would become the pastor as explained further in canon 1423 p. 2. We might repeat here the fine distinction of Father Augustine O. S. B. as to the different kinds of union possible here.[40] A parish may be united to a moral person *plenissimo jure* when not only the administration of the parish is given to the moral person but the whole territory of the parish is separated from the diocese. This happens with an abbey *nullius (sc. dioeseseos)* having its territory separated entirely from the jurisdiction of the Bishop of the rest of that locality. Such abbeys *nullius* not having at least three parishes are ruled by particular norms and do not come under the provisions

39 Bouix, De Jure Reg. II-45, apud Smith, op. cit. 504.
40 Op. cit. II-515.

of the New Code in Lib. II tit. VII cap. X.[41] We have no abbey *nullius* with only one parish in this country and we strongly doubt whether they will be found in any of the countries where diocesan consultors have hitherto been found. The Benedictine Abbey *nullius* of North Carolina embraces several counties and is therefore more like an independent diocese and is so considered in law.[42] It is evident that to dismember a diocese which is a major benefice, to create an abbey *nullius* of anykind is reserved to the Holy See entirely and the diocesan consultors have no direct voice in the matter.[43]

The second species of union and the one with which we are concerned here is *pleno jure* and it takes place when a moral person (even non-collegiate as a seminary for the canon does not distinguish) obtains permanent possession and administration of a parish in things both spiritual and temporal. When only the temporal or only the spiritual administration is entrusted to the moral person or even if both but not permanently the union is *semipleno jure*. The reference in canon 452 p. 1 to canon 1423 p. 2 merely states what unions are prohibited to the Ordinary. Thus it mentions specifically his inability to unite the parish with the capitular or the episcopal *mensa*.[44] (ecclesiastical property the funds of which go to the support of the chapter or the hishop respectively, it is therefore a species of benefices not hitherto had in this country. Possibly our system of *cathedracticum*[45] would answer the new definition of the endowment of a benefice) The Bishop is equally unable to unite the parish to a monastery or to any church of the religious or any moral person in general. The rest of the paragraph does not apply to this country for dignities are had only in cathedral chapters while collegiate churches are also unknown here. The reference to the cathedral church is also out of much practical import-

41 Can. 319 p. 1.
42 Can. 215 p. 2.
43 Can. 215 p. 1.
44 For definition of mensa cf. Boudinhon, Cath. Enc. X-194.
45 Cath. Enc. III-441. art. Cathedraticum.

ance to us because it refers rather to the revenues of the cathedral chapter which we do not have.

All the above mentioned acts are unions of benefices and hence in addition to a special permission of the Holy See dispensing from the prohibition of canons 452 and 1423 the advice of the diocesan consultors is required as already established in the preceding section in our commentary on canon 1428. This of course is to be taken to mean that such a consultation is to be held before such a petition is sent to Rome for their advice would be useless after the Holy See has already granted the permission. Father Augustine O. S. B.[46] provides a fine explanation of the entire procedure to be followed by the Bishop and the religious order to whom the Bishop desires to entrust the parish. Thus Father Augustine O. S. B. advises that mention be made in the petition forwarded to Rome that the advice of diocesan consultors has already been taken.

One might however be inclined to advance an objection from the peculiar form of canon 456 and from the apparent contradiction in the Code speaking of both religious pastors and religious vicars. The objection might be that what we have hitherto said is correct where the parish is united say with a college in the hands of a religious community or even when the parish is given over to a monastery but it does not seem readily evident that these provisions would apply to small parishes in charge of which there may be only one or even two religious but not enough to form a *domus formata*.[47] Is giving over a parish to one religious an union such as discussed in this article? We are constrained to admit a certain difficulty in solving this objection but all of the commentaries upon the New Code consulted by the writer if not explicitly at least implicitly seem to teach that there can not be giving over a parish to the religious except in this form of union. As one eminent canonist puts it even when only one religious is to be found in

46 Op. cit. II-515.
47 Can. 488 n. 50.

charge of a parish the habitual pastor there is the order or congregation of which he is the member. In other words even in such a case we have the union of the parish with another moral person in this case a collegiate person and that is the religious order or congregation, and as an union *pleno jure* is regulated by all the rules here expounded.

Further objection arises from the requirement of canon 452 p. 2 that in parishes united to a moral person and therefore all parishes entrusted to the religious there be constituted a "*vicarius paroecialtis*" that is the actual pastor should not be strictly called "*parochus*" and yet canon 454 p. 5 speaks of religious "*parochi.*" This difficulty is deepened when we turn to canon 471 p. 3 and there find mention of a religious vicar who is compared with the religious pastor of canon 454 p. 5 but clearly is not the same person. The only possible explanation which the writer can offer without admitting a species of entrusting a parish to the religious without the formality of an union is that the "*parochus religiosus*" is the same as the "*vicarius paroecialis*" but is called "*parochus*" because of his great similarity with the secular pastors. In such a supposition it would then be possible to restrict the "*vicarius paroecialis religiosus*"" of canon 471 p. 3 to cases where the moral person holding the parish is not the religious order proper but say a hospital in the care of a religious order. Certainly Father Augustine O. S. B.[48] understands the religious "*parochus*" and the "*vicarius*" as the same. Canon 456 is then interpreted by Father Augustine O. S. B. to include not only union *pleno jure.*[49] Even a *semipleno jure* union is reserved to the Holy See if by it is meant administration for a time only and hence there is no difference with the general requirement of Apostolic permission.[50] However we must leave to others to explain better the relation of religious to parishes, for

48 Op. cit. II-520.
49 Op. cit. II-525.
50 Can. 1423 p. 3.

us it will be sufficient that whenever it is an union whether *pleno* or *semipleno jure* it will require besides the Apostolic indult the advice of diocesan consultors in virtue of canon 1428. Even if we have to admit as possible entrusting parishes to religious without the formality of an union then the permission of the Holy See will also be necessary because dispensation would be required from the law of 1442, for the rest where the common law does not reach the old conciliar law will still remain and therefore in practice whatever we assume as the canonical explanation of the point it is certain that the consultors must be asked for their advice and permission from the Holy See be obtained before a parish can be given to the religious. Societies which are not strictly religious[51] will also be bound by canon 454 p. 1 if such an union be not admitted there is a *lacuna* in the law for otherwise there would be no formality required by the Bishop to entrust a parish to their care.

ARTICLE IV.

Their advice required for the appointment of Seminary Deputies.

Of the three Plenary councils constantly considered in this work only the Baltimore Council legislated in regard to this fourth case requiring the advice of the diocesan consultors i. e. the appointment of deputies for the diocesan seminary. The Sydney and Latin-American councils have no mention of this. The New Code retains this provision and therefore the advice of consultors in the appointment of these deputies will be obligatory now not only in the United States but in every diocese where diocesan consultors are found.

Recognizing that in proper early training of the clergy lay the best method for the reformation of the clerical life the Council of Trent devoted considerable attention

51 Can. 673.

to seminaries. In its twenty-third session (cap. 18 de ref.) the council decreed the establishment of a seminary in every diocese or at least in every province. For the external government of these diocesan seminaries two commissions were to be instituted, one for the temporal, the other for the spiritual administration of the seminary and the bishop was obliged to seek the advice of these commissions in matters concerning the seminary. The Third Plenary Council of Baltimore[52] adapted this Tridentine legislation to the circumstances of this country and decreed the establishment for every seminary whether diocesan or provincial, minor or major, of two similar committees, one for the spiritual, the other for the temporal management of the seminary. The chief modification of the Baltimore council was in the number of the members of these committees, the council admiting even one deputy for each commission, if no more be possible, whereas Trent required two as the very least on each commission. For the provincial seminaries these deputies were to be chosen by the Bishops of the province *collegialiter;* for the diocesan seminaries however they were to be chosen by the Bishop also but with the advice of his diocesan consultors. This legislation of course did not apply to seminaries entrusted to the care of a religious order or institute.

Whatever may have been the old legislation or the manner of its observance, we have now in the New Canon the explicit provision of canon 1359 laying down in clear terms the obligation of establishing in all diocesan seminaries two commissions or bodies of deputies, the one for discipline i. e. for the spiritual, internal management of the seminary, the other for the administration of the temporalities. This prescription like any other canon in the New Code is of universal application and hence affects all diocesan seminaries. It is still the desire of the Church that each diocese possess its own sem-

52 N. 178-179.

inary.[53] If the bishop sends his young candidates for the priesthood to another diocesan seminary this does not make that seminary provincial for inter-diocesan or regional seminaries are only those which have been so constituted by the Holy See. Such of course have then their own regulations approved by the Holy See.[54] Diocesan seminaries but in charge of religious very probably do not come under the requirement of canon 1359 both by reason of comparison with the old law which must guide us always in interpreting the new and because they may perhaps be included under the provisions of canon 1357 p. 1 which establishing the right and duty of the Bishop to oversee all that concerns the seminary excepts the case where the Holy See has established other norms. As it required at least a tacit or indirect understanding with the Holy See before a seminary could be entrusted to the religious most likely they all possess such peculiar norms.

These committees are to consist each of two priests chosen by the Bishop with the advice in our case of the diocesan consultors.[55] Formerly the commission for the spiritual management of the seminary was by common law to consist of two canons of the cathedral chapter.[56] The commission for the temporalities consisted of four members, two canons and two other priests from the city. One-half of the members of these commissions were appointed by the Bishop himself the other by the chapter. To-day all that is required is that the deputies be priests and all are appointed solely by the Bishop but with the *advice of the diocesan consultors* in our country. By analogy with the old law there can be nothing to prevent the appointment of diocesan consultors to the position also of the deputies of the seminary for paragraph 3 eliminating several classes of priests from this office does not mention the members of the cathedral chapter

53 Can. 1354 p. 1.
54 Can. 1357 p. 4.
55 Can. 1359 p. 2.
56 Ferreres op. cit. II-338.

or the diocesan consultors. The duration of their term of office is for six years but for their removal before the term of office lapses the Bishop requires only a grave cause nor is he strictly obliged to consult his body of diocesan consultors although this should be done in keeping with the practice on their appointment.

ARTICLE V.

Pro-synodal examiners and parish-priest consultors appointed with the advice of diocesan consultors.

The next case requiring the advice of consultors in Baltimore legislation was the selection of a new consultor and of the so-called pro-synodal examiners.[57] Of the advice or consent necessary in the selection of a new consultor to fill a vacancy sufficient has been said in chapter IV of this work. We can therefore directly take up the appointment of pro-synodal examiners. The Sydney council requiring an annual synod had no necessity for another formality for the election of examiners. The Latin-American council established a similar legislation as that of Baltimore but required an apostolic indult in addition.[58]

Synodal examiners are of Tridentine institution[59] and their specific duty was to conduct the concursus or the competitive examinations for vacant parishes. Examinations of candidates for Holy Orders, for approval for hearing confessions were not their specific duties although they could be entrusted to synodal examiners. Their name is due to the fact that ordinarily they are to be chosen in a diocesan synod If for any reason they were chosen out of synod then they were wont to be called pro-synodal examiners. When the Bishop could appoint a pro-synodal examiner he required always the consent of the cathedral chapter.

57 N. 20-50.
58 N. 245-40.
59 Sess. 24 c. 18 de ref.

In the United States the appointment of examiners was recommended by the Second Plenary Council of Baltimore but their duties were not those of synodal examiners of common law. When the Third Plenary Council instituted permanent rectorships, which came most closely to the notion of a canonical parish, it ordered also the institution of at least six examiners in each diocese to conduct the examinations for these permanent rectorships.[60] The council did not call them synodical examiners but examiners of the clergy yet the general name was attached sometimes to our examiners also. The examiners were also to be appointed in the diocesan synod with the advice of the assembled clergy. If the Bishop wished to appoint them out of synod he required permission from the Holy See to do so, and having obtained this leave he could proceed to their appointment but then with the advice of the diocesan consultors. Those so appointed were wont also to be styled the pro-synodal examiners.

The decree *"Maxima Cura"* of Aug. 20, 1910 changed in important particulars the discipline regarding synodal examiners and as it was of universal application it abrogated also the contrary prescriptions of the Baltimore council. Under the provisions of the decree *"Maxima Cura"* to appoint synodal examiners out of synod the *consent* of the chapter and here of the diocesan consultors was required,[61] as also it was required to fill a vacancy occurring in the board of examiners between synods.[62]

In the New Code the substance of the decree *"Maxima Cura"* is retained except that now not consent of the diocesan consultors but only their *advice* is required. Synodal examiners are still ordinarily to be chosen in the diocesan synod with the approval of the clergy gathered there, but if one should die or lose his office in any other manner the vacancy is filled by the appointment

60 b. n. 23-26.
61 S. C. Cons. c. 4 p. 3.
62 Ibid. p. 2.

of a pro-synodal examiner chosen by the Bishop alone with the advice of diocesan consultors. Where the synods are not convoked at the regular decennial period required[63] or if it be not at all held since the synodal examiners hold office only for ten years, at the expiration of that time new ones must be appointed out of synod if none is to be held soon, and then the rules given above for vacancies are to be observed i. e. the examiners are constituted by the Bishop but with the advice of diocesan consultors.

This will be the proper place to consider the relation of diocesan consultors to the appointment of parish-priest consultors and to the removal of both the synodal examiners and the parish-priest consultors. Being an institution promulgated for the first time by the decree "*Maxima Cura*" there is no mention of parish-priest consultors in any of the former particular legislations. Any foreshadowing of this institution observed by some authors does not concern us here. Parish-priest consultors are not to be confounded with diocesan consultors. They are parish priests called consultors because their duty is to advise the bishop in some of the processes concerning the administrative removal of parish priests. They might loosely be called an appeal board, as indeed they were styled in some dioceses, for in the "*Maxima Cura*" this was their only duty to revise as the board of appeal the acts of the removal of a pastor who has filed recourse against the plan. In the New Code their duties are somewhat more extended. Two of their number must be consulted when an irremovable parish priest takes recourse againts a decree of removal[64] and when any parish priest files objections to his transfer.[65]

Parish priest consultors like the synodal examiners are ordinarily to be selected in a synod[66] by the vote of the clergy present on the candidates presented by the Bishop. Like the synodal examiners they hold their office until the next synod but after ten years their term

63 Can. 356.
64 Can. 2153 p. 1.
65 Can. 2165.
66 Can. 385 p. 1.

of office[67] lapses and hence new consultors called pro-synodal parish priest consultors must be elected by the Bishop out of synod but with the advice of the diocesan consultors. The *"Maxima Cura"* required consent but this is now changed. The same is true in filling a vacancy in an unexpired term.

As the synodal examiners were elected for life there was no legislation in our councils for their removal. In the *"Maxima Cura"* the term of office for both synodal examiners and parish priest consultors was set at five years if a synod did not intervene. Within that time they could only be removed with the consent of the chapter or our board of diocesan consultors.[68] In the New Code consent in this matter is abrogated as it is also in their appointment. Canon 388 explicitly states that neither the synodal examiners nor the parish priest consultors can be removed during their term of office except for a grave cause and with the *advice* of the chapter or our diocesan consultors. In passing we may note that the new law generally has modified the former requirements of the consent of the cathedral chapter but has perhaps increased the number of cases where the Bishop is obliged to seek the advice of various persons. More freedom of action is therefore given to the bishop without eliminating the good that comes from taking the advice of other prudent men. Concluding this chapter we sum up; the *advice* of diocesan consultors is now required in the appointment of synodal examiners and parish priests consultors out of synod, in filling the vacancies of either class and in their removal for cause.

ARTICLE VI.

Their function in relation to the alienation of ecclesiastical property.

We come now to the sixth and the last case of diocesan consultors' advice enumerated in the general decree

67 We use the term office here in its wider acceptation equivalent to the latin "munus."
68 S. C. Cons. Aug. 20, 1910, c. 4 p. 5.

of Baltimore Council on this subject. Other cases were specified in scattered points of the Acts of this great council. We refer now to alienation of church property. In this matter we have the most important duty of diocesan consultors under the common law for in this case not only the advice but the *consent* of consultors is required.

Alienation as used in this connection signifies the act of conveying or transferring to another ecclesiastical property in any form. It is used broadly and hence signifies not only the transfer of the title to the property by sale but also the transfer of the use or the usufruct of a thing (locatio)[69] or the conveying of any right *in re (hypotheca-mortgage)*.[70] It includes any sacrifice of rights which exposes the object to loss or even makes the object become deteriorated in value hence donations, sales, exchanges or purchases of new property, compromises; the giving up of acquired rights of any kind, mortgages and other incumbrances upon property, the imposition of new taxes etc. are all species of alienation. Transfer of property from one ecclesiastical institution to another is included in this term.[71] According to Smith[72] it includes all property real and personal belonging not only to churches but even to such charitable institutions as hospitals, asylums, etc.

As the Church is only a moral person legally she is a minor, to quote Wernz,[73] whose property must be taken care of by the prelates who are her administrators. No one therefore, can dispose of the Church's goods validly without a proportionate cause. To safeguard the Church's rights in this matter canon law has introduced a number of solemnities and especially the requirement of the permission of proper ecclesiastical authorities coupled with the consent of the interested parties, as well

69 Called by Slater "bailment." Cf. Manual of Moral Theol. I-539.
70 Wernz, op. cit. III, n. 154.
71 Id. III-156.
72 Op. cit. p. 514.
73 Op. cit. III-157.

as that of the cathedral chapter. The goods that required these formalities were especially irremovable property and even removable property which could be preserved although custom has given free alienation of articles of small value.

In this country alienation of ecclesiastical property was regulated by the Third Plenary Council of Baltimore[74] and a decree of the Sacred Congregation of the Propaganda dated Sept 25, 1885. Much greater freedom was given to our bishops in this regard and only when the property exceeded the sum of $5,000 in value was it required that they first take the advice of diocesan consultors and then seek leave from the Holy See. The Sydney Council had almost identical legislation except that it required the advice of consultors in writing,[75] Its limit of the bishop's power of alienation was 200 pounds sterling. The Latin-American Council established $1,000 or 5.000 francs as the limit.[76] At least in the United States however the Holy See on the request of the bishops gathered in Council granted an indult for ten years dispensing the bishops from requiring in each case the permission of the Holy See. This indult was renewed at stated intervals and is now still in force.

What now is the legislation of the New Code in this regard ? The question is treated in Lib. III, tit. 29. In the first place we are expressly informed by canon 1533 that the formalities established are required in any contract as a result of which the condition of the church would be in a worse state than before. It therefore signifies alienation in the widest possible meaning of the term similarly as explained by the older writers. Secondly it refers only to property real or movable which can be preserved *(quae servando servari possunt)*[77] The words are exactly the words of the famous constitution of Paul II *"Ambitiosa"*, issued in 1468. Therefore all the old in-

74 N. 20-60.
75 N. 32.
76 N. 245.
77 Can. 1530. A good article on the question of alienation will be found in the Irish Ecclesiastical Record of 1914 p. 637.

terpretations as to what can be preserved and what not retain their full value. The fruits of a land as crops are the best example of what is not subject to these formalities.

The primary conditions required in alienation need not detain us long. They are as enumerated in canons 1530-1531 1) that a valuation by experts be made in writing of the object to be alienated, 2) that there be a just cause for alienation viz: urgent necessity, evident utility of the Church or of piety (e. g. to help the poor), 3) that proper precautions to be prescribed by the Superior for each particular case be taken lest the Church suffer any harm, 4) that the object be sold at not less than its appraised value, 5) that so far as possible it be sold at public auction to the highest bidder and the money thus realized be safely and profitably invested or deposited. But most important of all is the prescription of canon 1530 p. 1 n. 3 requiring the permission of the proper superior. This legitimate superior is solely the Holy See[78] when the object to be alienated is precious (i. e. articles of value because of their art, historical associations or rare material from which they were made). The same Holy See must be approached when the property exceeds in value the sum of 30,000 lire or francs. If the property is below 1,000 lire or francs in value then the permission of the local Ordinary is sufficient who however must consult the Council for the Administration of Church property which is prescribed in canon 1520 unless the object is of very little value. In addition he must always have the consent of the interested parties e. g. the superiors of a hospital etc.

Where however the value of the property or object exceeds the sum of 1,000 lire or francs but is below 30,000 lire or francs then in addition to the counsel or consent required in the preceding paragraph the Ordinary in this case must obtain the *consent* of the cathedral chapter and therefore in our regions of the diocesan consultors.

78 Can. 1532.

This is one of the few cases in which the *consent* of the diocesan consultors is required for the very *validity* of the act.[79] Of itself therefore this provision is much more stringent than that of the particular councils viz: Baltimore, Sydney and Latin-America. Yet this is a law which is clearly in opposition to the prescriptions of the three councils and in this conflict the superior law of the Code must prevail in virtue of canon 6n. 1. Apart therefore from the indults some of the bishops enjoy their power in this matter has been considerably curtailed. But the question now arises does the Bishop require the consultors' advice or consent when he asks the Holy See for permission to alienate property over 30,000 lire or francs in value? To the writer, *salvo meliori judicio* it seems that under the *common law* no further consent or advice is then required. In the first place there is no such limitation in the section of the canon prescribing the requisite permission of the Holy See and *"ubi lex non distinguit nec nos distinguere debemus."* Again we are to interpret the New Code in the light of the old law[80] but in the former common law the consent of the chapter in such cases was only required when the property belonged to the chapter itself which then of course was one of the interested parties whose consent is always required.[81] In other cases where the permission of the Holy See was to be obtained no further consent of the chapter was required. The condition of asking the consultors' advice was appended by the Holy See to its indults for alienation but that was bcause the indult itself was an exception from the common law and therefore some added precautions were only reasonable. We therefore venture to hold that by common law to alienate property above 30,000 lire or francs in value no previous advice or consent of the consultors is necessary although of course it is to be earnestly recommended. But this must be stressed, this is true in the *common* law only.

79 Can. 105.
80 Can. 6, n. 20, 40.
81 Bargilliat, Pralectiones Jur. Can. n. 975. Smith, op. cit. p. 516, Wernzz, op. cit. III-165.

Since the requirement of the consultors' advice in this matter is not contrary to the general law but merely in addition to it these laws of the Plenary Councils will stand in virtue of canon 22. Likewise the prescriptions of the particular indults granted by the Holy See will still oblige[82] but the sum established as the limit of the Bishop's power without the intervention of the consultors must be corrected to be in conformity with the New Code. Where therefore the Sydney council established 200 pounds sterling as the limit of the Bishop's freedom of alienating this must now be corrected to 1,000 lire or about 40 pounds without the consent of diocesan consultors and up to 30,000 lire or about 1,200 pounds sterling with the consent of the consultors, and only above this amount will it be required now to ask the permission of the Holy See but before asking for this by the law of Sydney Councils the Australian bishops will be required to ask their consultors advice in writing. For the United States the former limit for the Bishop's free power of alienation was by Baltimore law $5,000; above that they could alienate also in virtue of the indult but with the advice of the consultors. The indult dispensing from the obligation of recurring to the Holy See in single instances will remain in force in virtue of canon 4 but the other provisions must be corrected to the norms of canon 1532 so that the Ordinaries are free to alienate Church property without consulting any one only when the object is of very small value *("minimi momenti")*, otherwise he is to consult his diocesan council for the administration of church property. When the value exceeds 1,000 lire or francs our Ordinaries must in conformity with the common law take the additional advice of their diocesan consultors. When the sum exceeds 30,000 lire they are in contrast to the common law still enabled to alienate without recurring to the Holy See but with the obligation contained in the indult of taking their consultors' advice. The original indult is found with the

82 Can. 4.

Acts of the Third Plenary Council[83] and it was last extended on July 31, 1916 for another ten years. In other words until July 1926 or until the Holy See ordains otherwise our bishops can alienate property of any value with the obligation only of filing a report to the Holy See at the end of every three years and of obtaining the advice of diocesan consultors when the amount exceeds 1.000 lire.

Two questions suggest themselves here. In the first place what is to be taken as the standard, the current rate of exchange value of the various monetary units, or is it the normal rate of exchange recognized by governments. We are confident that the latter is meant i. e. the rate agreed upon by the governments for their international dealings as in the postal service. Therefore where 30,000 at the fluctuating rate of exchange at present might have meant only about $1,200 at the standard rate of the postal union it would mean $6,000 and this standard is to be followed. Certainly the Code meant to stand unchanged for centuries and did not intend to consider the daily fluctuation of money value. For this country therefore should the indult be withdrawn by common law the Bishop will require only the diocesan administration council's advice in sums below $200; from that sum to $6,000 he would require in addition the *consent* of diocesan consultors; above that sum a specific license would be required from the Holy See. In the meantime while the indult is still in force the Bishop must obtain the advice of the diocesan council of administration when the sum is not much below $200 for while we would be inclined to call this sum *minimi momenti* in our country still there is no evading the prescriptions of canon 1532 p. 2. Above that sum or rather above $250 because we may accept the more favorable exchange value of francs, the Bishop must obtain the consent of both the diocesan council of administration and that of the diocesan consultors. The consent of the interested

83 P. ciii.

parties is always required whatever be the amount. But here the other question arises. Under the common law above 30,000 lire or francs ($7,500) the Ordinary merely seeks the permission of the Holy See without the necessary formality of consulting the diocesan council of administration or the board of diocesan consultors. By the indult however our Bishops are dispensed from seeking permission in individual cases but require the advice of diocesan consultors. If our bishops should therefore wish to alienate a property say $10,000 in value in virtue of the indult nothing else would be required but the advice of the diocesan consultors. But if they wish to alienate a smaller amount say $5,000 they must observe the prescriptions of canon 1532 p. 2 and obtain the *consent* of both the diocesan council of administration and of the diocesan consultors. This is an anomalous situation yet the writer does not see how it can be evaded except by a new and broader indult from the Holy See. Of course there is the argument *"Qui potest plus potest et minus"* but in the face of the clear provisions of canon 1532 p. 2 the writer cannot see how the indult would avail. The indult dispenses according to the interpretation of Smith[84] from the obligation of recurring to the Holy See in each individual instance and not outright from the solemnities of law although in the mind of the writer the original indult would lend itself also to that interpretation. The safer course to follow therefore is for the Bishop to observe the prescriptions of the New Code and obtain the *consent* of both the diocesan council of administration and of the diocesan consultors at least in the amounts up to $6,000. Above that amount he may proceed with the advice only of the diocesan consultors. But if a bishop should even in the smaller amounts proceed with the advice only of the diocesan consultors, the writer would not venture to declare such action clearly invalid. We think this would be a most reasonable question to submit to Rome for a solution.

We may also note here that if the consent or even the

84 Op. cit., 517.

advice of the consultors be required, the nature of the question demands that the consultors before being asked for their advice or consent, as the case may be should be given an opportunity for full discussion and investigation of the sufficiency of the causes for alienation. It should be also noted that leasing of church property is specifically mentioned in canon 1541 as following the rules here laid down for the various formalities in alienation and the term of lease is not less than nine years. When the term is less than nine years then it follows the norms for alienation but of the next lower class. Therefore by common law the consent of diocesan consultors will be required for the lease below nine years in which the yearly rent exceeds $6,000 and in longer terms for all yearly rents above $200. Note too that if the object alienated is divisible the bishop must inform those whose consent he requires how much of the property or object has been alienated before and this is for the validity of the new consent.

A very severe penal sanction is established by the Code for those transgressing the laws in regard to alienation. It is found of course in the Fifth Book of the Code (can. 2347) and establishes not only the obligation of repairing any harm that may have been wrought by him who has presumed to alienate ecclesiastical goods or has given his consent to such alienation contrary to provisions of canon 1532 the Ordinary and the other clerics invalid, (for us the diocesan consultors), are to pay a sum double the amount of property so alienated to the Church or pious institute that was injured by the action. It is to be noted however that this canon uses the word "*praesumpserit*" and therefore any ignorance except affected ignorance would remove the imputability and therefore excuse from the penalty. (can. 2229).

Briefly then the conclusions of the writer are these. The *consent* of diocesan consultors is by common law required in all alienations exceeding the sum of $200 in value but not above the sum of $6,000; of above $6,000, the permission of the Holy See is required. It seems that our Ordinaries can only use their indult when the sum is in excess of this $6,000 and then they apparently are only bound to the *advice* of diocesan consultors. The *consent* of diocesan consultors is similarly required in leases under nine years for property over $$6,000 and for all terms for all other sums. But as leases are only a species of alienation our Ordinaries can apply their indult on similar terms for leases that require only the advice of diocesan consultors, when the yearly rent exceeds $6,000.

ARTICLE VII.

Consultors in reference to imposition of new taxes.

The last case enumerated by the Baltimore decree on the duties of consultors in which their advice was required is the question of imposing new taxes for the Bishop. The other councils have no similar legislation, nor was it originally adopted by the Fathers of the Third Plenary Council of Baltimore for according to Dr. S. B. Smith[85] this part of the decree[86] was inserted by the Sacred Congregation of the Propaganda when the acts and decrees of the Council were submitted to it according to law for its revision. The words of this prescription were "*Item praehabito consilio consultorum necessarius erit recursus ad S. Sedem in singulis casibus in quibus agitur de imponenda nova taxa pro episcopo, quae excedat limites a canonibus constitutas*" Dr. Smith in his commentary[87] on this part of the Baltimore decree feared to advance any explanation of the meaning of these words. But in another part of his work[88] he does give us his view on the meaning of this provision which we shall study at greater length. Fr. Nilles S. J.[89] the only other commentator in this matter does not give a direct

85 Op. cit. I-p. 518.
86 Conc. Plen. Balt. III, n. 20 in fine.
87 I. c.
88 P. 391 n. 610.
89 P. 62.

answer but illustrates what is meant by showing where in common law the consent of the chapter was required for the imposition of certain new taxes.

In the old legislation there were various taxes imposed by the Church upon the faithful both the lay and the clerics. There were thus the tithes,[90] offerings of first fruits,[91] and other offerings in general but these were rather applied to the lay members of the Church. Other taxes were imposed upon clerics or ecclesiastical property as such, especially benefices. Of such a kind were especially the census, the so-called extraordinary exactions and procuration or the hospitality extended to the bishop on the occasion of his canonical visitation.[92] Our cathedraticum is one form of these tributes.[93] The census[94] is defined by Wernz as an annual sum of money that must be paid to the superior out of the income of an ecclesiastical benefice or institute. The power of bishops to impose such a census was limited to cases expressly determined by common law. The seminary tax, the cathedraticum were expressly permitted. Exactions are called by Wernz those taxes which are imposed on extraordinary occasions. Authors do not distinguish sharply between the two classes of tributes. As an example of an extraordinary assessment may be some tax imposed for a charitable purpose e. g. a diocesan hospital. For such an assessment the consent of the chapter was necessary. The amount of our cathedraticum was chiefly regulated by diocesan synod,[95] perhaps then the prescriptions of the Baltimore council applied to cases where the bishop would attempt to impose a new tax for himself out of all proportion to the amount recognized by custom or synodal statute.

Whatever may have been the old law the new legislation is much more definite in this regard. In the first

90 Wernz, op. cit. III-211ss.
91 Id. n. 221.
92 Id. n. 223 ss.
93 Cath. Enc. XIV-322, art. "Subsidies."
94 Idem. III-533 art. "Census."
95 Idem. III-442 art. "Cathedraticum."

place it drops all the ancient names and uses the simple term of tax *(taxa)* or tribute *(tributum)*. The word tax is used more in the sense of a fee as for juridical expenses,[96] or for stole fees in connection with the administration of sacraments,[97] or ecclesiastical burial[98] or chancery fees[99] etc. More like the ancient census are the tributes especially the cathedraticum.[100]

In connection with the taxes in the strict signification just explained the *advice* of the chapter or of our diocesan consultors is only necessary in the following specific cases. It is the desire of the Code that in each diocese there be a standard schedule of offerings due for the various classes of funeral services.[101] The amount of these offerings if not already determined (e. g. by synodal statutes) the local Ordinary is to determine with the advice of the chapter or our diocesan consultors. We have been unable to discover any other case in the new legislation where the advice of the chapter or of the diocesan consultors is required by law in connection with some tax or tribute. According to canon 6 n. 1 therefore all the provisions of the old common law requiring the consent of the chapter in some of these cases must now be considered abrogated. But does the New Code also abrogate the decree of the Baltimore Council? *Salvo meliori judicio* we think it does because to us it seems to be opposed to canons 1504-1507 and no old particular law con now stand in opposition to the provisions of the Code. The whole question centers therefore in our mind as to what tax was meant in the Baltimore decree we have reference to.

We shall take this question up part by part. The ordinary taxes which the bishops could levy in the old legislation by whatever name we choose to style them were then divided into the new or the old. The old meant

96 Can. 909.
97 Can. 736.
98 Can. 1234.
99 Can. 59 p. 2, 1056.
100 Can. 1504.
101 Can. 1234-1235.

here a tax *(census antiquus)* which was expressly authorized by the general law.[102] Such were the *cathedraticum* and the seminary collections and both are expressly authorized in the New Code in canons 1504 and 1355 respectively. No consent therefore or advice even is required of the consultors in this connection although it should not be spurned.

Another form of the ordinary tax was the hospitality extended to the bishop on the occasion of his canonical visitation and was styled *"procuratio"*. This too is recognized by the New Code in canon 346 which specifies that the proper custom of the locality be observed. Provided therefore the proper mean be observed all these taxes as expressly permitted by the Code require no intervention of the diocesan consultors.

It was in regard to imposing new perpetual ordinary taxes or annual pensions that the Holy See was so opposed in the old legislation as to require a special license from the Holy See. Increase of the old taxes was placed in the same class. Most likely therefore it was this that the Holy See had in mind when it inserted the requirement of the advice of consultors and then permission from the Holy See for a new tax for the bishop. But today canon 1506 expressly states that the Ordinary can impose a tribute which from comparison with the preceding canon must mean a perpetual regular tribute without asking the advice or seeking the consent of any one. What was therefore formerly called the census or ordinary tax can now be legitimately imposed by the bishop although limited to the occasion of the foundation or consecration of the benefice or institute. But a freedom granted by the Code cannot be restricted by any former particular legislation and hence the Baltimore decree can no longer hold at least in this connection. The canon would perhaps find application in this country only with the consecration of some church in which case the Bishop might impose upon the well established parish a

102 Smith, op. cit. n. 609 ff.

certain regular tax to support e. g. the poorer missions of the dioceses.

More practical are the so-called extraordinary taxes, for instance a special assessment made to defray the expenses of the bishop's visit *ad limina.* This the bishop could impose even in the former legislation on his own authority where the constitution of Innocent XI did not obtain but only for a manifestly reasonable cause and with the consent of the chapter.[103] Not impossibly this form of taxation may have been in the mind of the Sacred Congregation of the Propaganda when it inserted the prescription on taxes in the Baltimore decree but today canon 1505 gives the Ordinary explicit power of imposing such extraordinary taxes upon all beneficiaries without any taking of advice provided only there be a special impelling need of the diocese and the tax be moderate. Here however we find a term that requires further consideration. The canon considers only beneficiaries as possible of taxation. What of conditions in this country? To us this is only another indication that the New Code does not consider it very possible to have ecclesiastical institutes or parishes which at least generally are not at the same time benefices. Taking the canon as it stands our bishops have no power to levy any such extraordinary assessment unless they admit our parishes are benefices. An argument from analogy (can. 20) we do not think would be quite sufficient to justify the bishop to tax parishes that are not benefices. One therefore who will refuse to acknowledge our parishes are benefices is necessarily driven to the conclusion that in that case the former legislation of Baltimore would stand with its requirement of the advice of consultors and recurrence to the Holy See. Dr. Meehan[104] however does not require leave of the Holy See in this case.

To summarize therefore in this confusing situation the following is to be accepted as the norm in the future.

103 Smith, op. cit. n. 609, II; Wernz, op. cit. III-224.
104 In the Cath. Enc. XIV-322, art. "Subsidies."

Holding as we do that the parishes are benefices we think the Code gives the bishops sufficient power to exact any reasonable though extraordinary assessment. As regards the old taxes the seminary tax is fixed to a maximum of 5%[105] while the cathedraticum must be moderate. The amount of the cathedraticum if not already regulated by custom can only be determined by the Bishops of a province assembled either in council or in the simple *conventus* in accordance with the prescriptions of the Code in canon 1504, 1507. While therefore we recommend that advice be always asked of the diocesan consultors in all these questions there is no such obligation by common law except in connection with defining the amount of a funeral offering. The Baltimore law we therefore consider abrogated as in opposition to the New Code unless one could imagine a tax for the bishop which would not be a *cathedraticum.*

ARTICLE VIII.

Their connection with changing the status of a parish.

Besides its general decree on consultors specifying cases where their advice was required the Baltimore council inserted the same requirement in some other decrees scattered throughout its acts. Among the first such was the requirement[106] that the bishops select certain churches in their diocese and appoint their rectors irremovable pastors. The selection of these parishes was to be made with the advice of the diocesan consultors. Likewise the selection of the first pastor to occupy such a parish was to be made by the bishop without a concursus but with the advice of his diocesan consultors.[107] The New Code has a legislation somewhat similar but also in certain respects directly contrary. Irremovable parishes cannot of course be rendered remov-

105 Can. 1356 p. 2.
106 N. 33.
107 N. 37.

able again except by permission of the Holy See.[108] To make a removable parish an irremovable one requries, as before the advice of the diocesan consultors. But, and here is the innovation, new parishes should be erected as irremovable parishes, and to erect them as removable parishes only the bishop requires not only peculiar circumstances making such an erection more expedient but also the advice of his diocesan consultors.[109] Our diocesan consultors must therefore be consulted in the erection of each new parish if the bishop desires his erection of the parish as a removable parish to be valid. We think too that the former requirement of the Baltimore council that the first rector of an irremovable parish be appointed with the advice of diocesan consultors is now to be considered abrogated. Our pastors whether removable or irremovable are all canonical pastors and hence are regulated by the regulations found in the Code and not by any particular legislation of Baltimore. Furthermore no particular law can limit the right of the bishop to appoint secular pastors without the intervention of diocesan consultors.[110]

The Baltimore law required also the advice of consultors[111] to determine the amount of the pension of an irremovable rector who has resigned or who has been removed on account of inculpable unfitness or inability for the proper discharge of the arduous duties of a rector. The Sydney council possessed a similar provision[112] The New Code provides differently for such cases. In the first place no pastor removable or irremovable is to be deprived of his office for mere inculpable inability to perform the duties of a pastor if the good of the parish can be provided for by what we might call a vicar-auxiliary as established in canon 475. Only where this is insufficient can the parish priest be removed but even then in the manner prescribed in canons 2147-2161 and then if

108 Can. 454 p. 3.
109 Ibidem.
110 Can. 455 p. 1.
111 N. 35.
112 N. 42.

the removed pastor can not hold any office or benefice whatever a pension is then to be given him to be determined by the Ordinary with the advice of those that took part in the process of removal i. e.either the parish priest consultors or the synodal examiners.[113] In this last case therefore the consultors are no longer asked for advice.

The Baltimore council also required the advice of the diocesan consultors in determining the amount of the pastor's salary, the amount of the *jura stolae* if done outside of synod and other similar questions. Thus in number 273 the council prescribed that for proper order the bishop should define in a synod the proper amount of a congruous salary to be paid to the rectors. But if the bishop preferred not to wait for a synod he was obliged to define this sum himself after taking the advice of his consultors. But where the mission was unable to pay the sum required the rector was obliged to accept less in which case the bishop was to judge but also with the advice of the diocesan consultors. Under no consideration was it to be permitted that the salary be taken out of the funds of the church already invested, i. e. provided the rector received enough to clothe and feed him. But the Bishop was not even obliged to supply these necessaries if with his consultors he should judge that the priest himself was seriously to blame for this want of the necessaries of life.

So far as pertains to the salary of the pastors we think that the legislation of the council remains in full force for there is no contrary law in the Code which would abrogate it. The Code does not take up anywhere *ex professo* the question of salaries. The necessaries of life are of course included in the title of ordination.[114] If our parishes are benefices there is a certain income connected with whatever constitutes the endowment *(dos)* of the parish.[115] Furthermore the pastor has a right to any offerings that he may receive by approved cus-

113 Can. 2154-2161.
114 Can. 979.
115 Can. 1472.

tom.[116] The legislation therefore of Baltimore in this regard is *praeter legem* and consequently not abrogated. As regards the *jura stolae* we have already discussed the question in article VII of this chapter. Their amount is now decided by the Bishops of the province assembled in council or in simple *conventus* with the subsequent approbation of the Holy See. To summarize therefore the duties of the diocesan consultors in connection with parishes or their rectors their advice is required to institute a new parish as a removable parish, to change a removable parish into an irremovable one and under the Baltimore law to determine the amount of the pastors' salaries and questions connected therewith.

ARTICLE IX.

NEW DUTIES

So far we have followed the legislation of the particular councils and especially that of Baltimore and have observed that most of these duties remain although the explanation of the source of these rights is different. Now we shall consider some of the new rights and duties acquired by the diocesan consultors by the promulgation of the New Code and the elevation in their status to that possessed by the cathedral chapter functioning as the senate of the bishop.

The advice of the chapter and hence too of our diocesan consultors, is now required by the bisop for the reservation of sins if this is done outside of diocesan synod. (Can. 859) An instruction of the Sacred Congregation of the Holy Office was issued July 13, 1916 establishing certain rules to be observed by the Ordinaries in reserving sins and this instruction is embodied almost without change in the New Code. (Lib. III, tit. IV, cap. II) The chapter refers principally to reservation of sins on their own account but reservation of sins with

116 Can. 463.

censures by the bishop are very probably also included in this chapter. For all such reservations therefore the New Code lays down the rule that the cases to be reserved should first be discussed in a diocesan synod. But if this be impossible then the Bishop must take advice of his diocesan consultors along with other prudent priests of the diocese as to what sins should be reserved.

A second new case of advice required of the diocesan consultors is given by the Code in canon 1292. It is prescribed there that for ordering an extraordinary public procession the Ordinary requires the advice of the chapter i. e. for us the advice of the diocesan consultors. The liturgical notion of a procession and its chief *ratio* is according to canon 1290 that of solemn supplication. For this reason in times of adversity or even for celebrating some happy event the Church sanctions the leading of a solemn procession to supplicate God for turning away the calamity or in thanksgiving for some great grace received. There are a number of occasions enumerated in the liturgical books when ordinary processions can be held but to conduct a solemn public procession outside of these days the Church requires first of all the permission of the Ordinary who however cannot decree such a procession except upon advice with his consultors, as to the reasonableness of the cause for such a solemn function.

A third new case of advice required of consultors is in connection with sacred furnishings *(sacra supellex)*. Where a church is very poor the Ordinary may permit that a moderate offering be required of priests celebrating Mass there *in proprium commodum* i. e. not attached to the parish but celebrating Mass for their own intention. It is not unfair to require that such priests make a slight contribution to the support of the poor church and to defray the expenses of supplying and keeping clean the sacred vestments and utensils. Canon 1303 p. 4 requires the Bishop to define what would be a reasonable offering preferably in the synod, but if not done in synod the Bishop is to settle the amount out of synod but with the advice of the chapter or in our case that of the diocesan consultors.

An innovation of some importance in the New Code is the council for the administration of church property which must be instituted in each diocese and whose members are to be elected with the advice of diocesan consultors. (Can. 1520) The Ordinary is the proper administrator of all church property in his diocese not specifically exempted and it is his task to observe by issuing even instructions if necessary, that this business be well ordered in conformity with the requirements of common law and local customs or regulations. To aid him in such a responsible duty the Code requires every Ordinary to institute in the episcopal city a Council for the Administration of Church Property This council is to consist of the bishop as the president and at least two other qualified members. From the language used it is evident that these members may be even laymen but what is especially desired is that they be acquainted with civil law. The institution of such a council is obligatory unless other provisions of equal value have been made either by particular law or by local custom. The members of this council are selected by the Bishop but with the advice of the diocesan consultors. Close relatives of the bishop are excluded from membership in this council.

There remains a case requiring the advice of the cathedral chapter which may and may not apply to this country. Under common law the cathedral church and the so-called episcopal *mensa* are constituted as benefices, wherefore they are moral persons and may be represented in trials. Their representative in such a case is the Ordinary who however for the liceity of his action requires the advice of his cathedral chapter or of the council of administration where the amount concerned is such as in case of alienation would require their consent. At present most likely we do not have any property which would go directly to the support of the cathedral church or the bishop so as to constitute an independent benefice distinct from the parochial benefices. If however such should be the case the Bishop to stand licitly in trial in defense of such property would require the advice of diocesan consultors where the amount involved exceeds $200.

There are other new provisions in the New Code but they are not requirements of their advice. Thus one of such new points is the prescription of canon 286 p. 3 requiring the convocation of diocesan consultors to a provincial council. These councils will now be important for the New Code obliges them to be held at least every twenty years.[117] Many duties are assigned to this council thus the stole fees mentioned in the previous article[118] are to be settled in such provincial councils. The Bishops, Abbots or Prelates *nullius* alone obtain a vote in the proceedings of the council but in addition to the bishops the boards of diocesan consultors of each diocese taking part in the council must be invited to send two representatives although these possess only an advisory vote. The presence of diocesan consultors at provincial councils should add much to the practical value of these assemblies as it gives the clergy an indirect representation and opportunity to make reasonable suggestions.

Another result of the parity now between consultors and the cathedral chapter in most matters is that the consultors like the chapter receive the letters of appointment of the new bishop by which act the bishop takes canonical possession of the diocese. Under the provisions of canon 334 the bishop newly appointed can exercise no jurisdiction in the see for which he is appointed until his apostolic briefs or letters are presented either by himself or by a procurator to the chapter of that diocese and with us to the body of diocesan consultors. Of course if the bishop has already been exercising jurisdiction as the Vicar-capitular he remains in that office but he does not attain the power of a bishop *sede plena* until he takes canonical possession of the diocese the

117 Can. 283.
118 Can. 1507.

same as any other bishop by presenting his letters of appointment to the diocesan consultors. The chancellor must be present to record the preceedings in authentic acts if the diocesan consultors have not their own secretary to perform this function.

In a similar way the diocesan consultors receive the letters of appointment of an Administrator Apostolic who takes charge of a diocese in which the see is still occupied.[119] The letters are presented to the bishop occupying the see if he is not out of his mind and also to the chapter i. e. with us to the diocesan consultors. But if the see happens to be vacant or the bishop be unable to receive such letters, either due to his enforced absence or to his mental or physical condition, then the Administrator Apostolic takes possession of the see in the same fashion as prescribed for the new bishop i. e. by presenting the letters to the consultors alone.

A coadjutor appointed to a see with the right of succession is to all purposes the same as a new bishop appointed for that see and hence he follows almost the same procedure. Such a coadjutor therefore presents his apostolic letters not only to the bishop occupying the see but also to the chapter, that is for us to the body of diocesan consultors.

This exhausts the list of the definite rights and duties of diocesan consultors with the see occupied. There remain however other references in the new legislation to cathedral chapters which while not directly applying to diocesan consultors, might perhaps be laudably imitated by them. Thus the Bishop is permitted to take two members of the cathedral chapter with him as his companions on the occasion of the canonical visitation of the diocese. While this canon (343 p. 2) is rather meant to show that he is not bound to select any particular priests he might well honor his board of diocesan consultors by asking two of their number to accompany him in this visitation. The prescription of canon 1009 re-

119 Can. 313.

quiring the presence of the canons of the cathedral at the general ordinations could also be imitated without however any obligation for it is clear that the chapter in that case attends rather as a college for more solemn worship and not so much as the senate of the bishop. The general ordinations are in the mind of the Church to be attended with the greatest possible solemnity and the presence of diocesan consultors in a body in imitation of the chapter would certainly add to the impressiveness of the scene.

For us in the United States there is one more function in which the consultors are asked for advice but not in the same relation as hitherto expounded. By a decree of the Sacred Consistorial Congregation dated July 25, 1916 a method of proposal was introduced in the selection of candidates for future appointments to the vacant bishoprics in the United States. Every two years the Bishops of each province are to meet and select several names of priests whom they regard as worthy of future promotion to the episcopate and send these to the sacred Consistorial Congregation. To obtain the fullest possible information in regard to each candidate the bishops should informally and secretly ask their diocesan consultors and irremovable rectors in reminiscence of the old method for their opinion on the candidates in mind.[120] In this function however they act not so much *ex officio* as honored priests of the diocese.

120 Augustine, op. cit. II-121; art. 2ss. of the decree.

CHAPTER X.

RIGHTS AND DUTIES *SEDE IMPEDITA* OR *SEDE VACANTE*.

So little is to be said about the duties of diocesan consultors *sede impedita* that it can best be treated in connection with their duties *sede vacante*. As already defined in the preceding chapter the see is called *impedita* when the proper bishop is unable to communicate with his diocesans even by letters whether this be due to imprisonment, relegation, exile or his own physical or mental disability.[1] Captivity may be due either to enemies of the state, as e. g. captivity by foreign troops, or carrying away by some barbarous tribes or even ordinary imprisonment by inimical civil authorities. Relegation is confinement to a given town, in this case however outside the diocese. When one is not only confined to a certain locality but entirely banished from the country his state is called exile.

In all these cases the administration of the diocese passes into the hands of the Vicar general or any other priest chosen by the bishop who may even delegate several for such purposes, not indeed *in solidum* but successively.[2] As the see is still juridically filled the Vicar-general in such a case exercises the ordinary power given him by law and in addition any other specific power which the Bishop might by a special mandate choose to delegate upon him. If a priest not the Vicar-general administer the diocese then he possesses only so much power as the Bishop specifically delegates to him. But what when even these men are impeded from the exercise of their office or the bishop fails to provide for the contingency. Let us suppose the bishop and the Vicar-

1 Can. 429 p. 1.
2 Ibidem. p. 2; Blat, op. cit. II-399.

general so imprisoned by the rabid civil authorities that the Bishop would be unable to communicate with any priest whom he might appoint his delegate to administer the see in the inability of both himself and the Vicar-general. In such a event the see is to all practical purposes vacant. The New Code for the first time makes a provision for such a case and allows the cathedral chapter and by consequence the diocesan consultors, to elect a temporary Vicar-capitular who is to notify the Holy See as soon as possible and in the meantime administer the see with the power of a Vicar capitular *sede vacante.* With us the proper Congregation to be notified would be the Sacred Consistorial Congregation which would then most likely appoint someone temporary Administrator Apostolic. It is to be noted that no Vicar capitular can be elected when the bishop is unable to exercise his duties by reason of a censure contracted. In such a state of affairs e. g. if a bishop should consecrate another bishop without a special permission from the Holy See and thus contract the suspension contained in canon 2370, the Vicar-general could not exercise jurisdiction because his power is suspended with that of the Bishop.[3] Swift recurrence to the Holy See is the only thing left in those peculiar circumstances but they of course will be rare. As to the procedure of electing the Vicar or the Administrator in this case the procedure is exactly the same as in the case of a vacancy and therefore we shall take up now the duties of consultors with the see specifically vacant.

In the first ages of the Church if a see became vacant its temporary administration passed into the hands of the nearest bishop.[4] But aready in the decretals of Gregory IX[5] was it estabished that the Cathedral chapter, then at its highest stage of development, should take over the administration of the vacant see. This administration the chapter exercised either directly or in-

3 Can. 371.
4 Bargilliat, op. cit. I, n. 799 ff; Wernz, op. cit. II-795.
5 C. 2, X, ne sede vacante, III, 9.

directly by the appointment of vicars who depended however entirely upon the chapter for their stay in that office.[6] This led to abuses which were corrected by the Council of Trent[7] which required the chapters to elect a Vicar-capitular to administer the see and this vicar to be elected within eight days after the vacancy has arisen was not any longer dependent upon the chapter for the tenure of his office. The law of Trent has been retained in substance to this very day.

The law in the New Code on this subject is to be found in chapter VI of the section we have so far been studying. (Lib. II. tit. VIII). There are few changes in this matter which would interest us. Canon 430 is important in our matter because it defines authentically when the see becomes actually vacant. It becomes vacant in the same four ways as any other irremovable ecclesiastical office can be lost i. e. by death, resignation, transfer and privation. To us it is of interest to determine the exact moment of legal vacancy.

The most ordinary origin of the vacancy of a see is the death of the Bishop. The moment this occurs the administration of the see passes into the hands of the cathedral chapter and consequently also in the hands of our diocesan consultors. As the vacancy of the see in this case is dependent upon the physical death of the bishop the chapter could validly exercise its jurisdiction even without possessing certain knowledge of the bishop's death but to exercise it *licitly* it must have received a certain and reliable news of his death. As Father Augustine O. S. B.[8] brings it out the certainty need not be juridical but one satisfying any prudent man. In case of serious doubt the Holy See is to be consulted but in the meantime the administration of the see remains in the hands it was in before e. g. the vicar-general. The chapter and hence our consultors cannot act until they have certain knowledge of the death of the Bishop.

6 Bargilliat, l. c.
7 Sess. XXIV, c. 16, de ref.
8 Op. cit. II-476.

Resignation of an episcopal see rarely occurs but when one takes place the procedure in its regard is clear. The see does not become vacant until the Holy See (in this case at least for us the Sacred Consistorial Congregation) accepts the resignation. Here however we must take especial note of the fundamental prescription found in canon 190 affecting all ecclesiastical offices not excepting the episcopate. It is that resignation does not take full effect until the one resigning receives certain notice of its acceptance. In our case therefore the chapter and diocesan consultors have no power until the bishop receives word that his resignation has been accepted.

More frequent will be the third method of a vacancy arising viz: through the transfer of the Bishop. In this case however the bishop remains temporarily in his former see as the Vicar-capitular *ipso facto* so appointed by the law and therefore neither the chapter nor the consultors receive any power at the moment of transfer. It is however important to them to know when the transfer has taken place because the see then being legally vacant the bishop same as any other Vicar-capitular must now seek the *consent* of the consultors in various cases to be shortly enumerated. The dispositions of the Code in the matter of the transfer of bishops is somewhat new. For us it is sufficient to know that the see becomes vacant not when the transfer has been announced in the Consistory, as was the former discipline, but only when the bishop is duly informed of these acts. Here too we think Father Augustine's interpretation[9] would be safe to follow, viz: that in this case as well as in case of deposition authentic, official news must be received before the see becomes juridically vacant. No press report or even a telegram from a friend would suffice.

The transferred bishop is obliged to take possession of his new see within four months but if he should fail to do this we do not think that he would lose his powers of a Vicar-capitular at the end of the four months. The day

9 Op. cit. II-478.

however he takes formal possession of the new see, that moment the former see becomes fully vacant and the administration passes into the hands of the chapter or the diocesan consultors as in case of death.

The last method of a vacancy arising will indeed be rare. We refer to the removal of the Bishop from his office. That a see may become vacant in this fashion the penalty must be very certainly intimated to the bishop. There will therefore be no difficulty in learning when the see becomes vacant in case of deposition. We must note however cases of tacit resignation *ipso jure* enumerated in canon 188. The provisions of this canon apply to all offices and therefore *per se* even to bishoprics. The only probable case of such tacit resignation with the bishop would be public apostasy and hence as a crime we treat of it here. It must be noted however that this must be public and certain. Ordinarily the Holy See may be expected to have provided for the case beforehand, if not it may generally be better to denounce the fact to the Holy See and only after the Holy See has deposed him should the chapter or the consultors take over the administration of the see. In rigor of the law however we think the chapter and the consultors could validly proceed to the election of a Vicar-capitular the moment such apostasy becomes notorious.

There are a few cases in law of privation *ipso facto* but scarcely one would be possible in practice. One elected a bishop is obliged by law to receive consecration within six months so that at the end of that period he would lose *ipso facto* his appointment.[10] It might therefore occur that a bishop would take possession of his see even before his consecration and then omitting to receive consecration in the appointed time, he would fall under the penalty of canon 2398 and lose his office. It is to be noted however that even penalties specified in law as *ipso facto incurrenda* require a declaratory sentence and therefore as far as concerns us an authentic decree of the Holy See must always intervene.

10 Wernz, op. cit. II, n. 539 Scholion II.

In cases of resignation and deposition most probably the Holy See will immediately make other provisions for the administration of the vacant see and hence occasions for the chapter or the consultors to exercise their power of jurisdiction may not in those cases always arise. But even in cases of vacancy by death or by the transferred bishop's occupation of the new see, the Holy See may sometimes have already provided another administrator. Thus it is specifically provided in canon 431 that where there already is an Administrator Apostolic, as where the former bishop has been physically or mentally disabled, the jurisdiction of the diocese passes into his hands and not into that of the chapter. The same is true where there is a coadjutor *cum jure successionis*.[11] But if the coadjutor is not so specifically named he has no power in the vacant diocese even if he is auxiliary to the see and not to the person of the Bishop alone. In most cases however we presume that the Holy See nominating a coadjutor to the see would also specify in the letters that he should administer the see in its vacancy.

When therefore the see becomes certainly vacant and the Holy See has not made any other provisions the administration of the diocese passes over to the chapter. In virtue of canon 427 this same power most certainly passes now into the board of diocesan consultors where they and not the cathedral chapter are found. This is probably the greatest practical innovation of the Code as affecting our diocesan consultors. It was the former custom in this country for the bishops to appoint some one the administrator of the see before their death. The consultors nowhere had any power in the vacant diocese except to present along with the irremovable rectors the three names for the new bishop and to assist the Administrator with the same advice they were called upon to offer to the bishop. The importance therefore of this change cannot be over estimated. Certain writers have indeed been led to deny this power to our diocesan con-

11 Can. 355 p. 1.

sultors but fortunately Rome has authoritatively settled this question by a decree of the Sacred Consistorial Congregation dated Feb. 22, 1919. This declaration answered specifically to doubts proposed by the Apostolic Delegate for this country that the provisions of Baltimore councils in this matter are now abrogated and hereafter the disposition of canon 427 (applying to consultors the same power as possessed by the chapter) are to be absolutely applied with the exceptions specified in the decree. The exception was this that some of our dioceses still possess only two consultors and it seemed somewhat incongruous to give them the power of electing the administrator of the vacant diocese and therefore the Sacred Congregation has thus decreed. Where there are less than five consultors the provisions of canon 427 will in this matter be not applied to them but the Administrator of the vacant diocese will instead be appointed by the Metropolitan or the senior suffragan bishop with the approbation of the Delegate. But this provision holds only for three years and it is specifically forbidden for a bishop to name his own administrator. It also must be remembered that this decree is a purely local legislation and hence consultors in other countries no matter what their number possess the power of electing the administrator unless the Holy See extended similar legislation to their countries.[12] It shows too how important it is to raise the number of consultors to the one specified by the Code.

The boards of consultors therefore in this country numbering at least five members and in other countries all bodies of diocesan consultors take full charge of the see upon it becoming certainly vacant. Their most important duty at that time is to elect one who will administer the diocese in their name although not revocable by them, i. e. they are to elect a Vicar-capitular. Until they elect this vicar-capitular or administrator as we have been accustomed to call the person the diocesan consult-

12 Irish Ecclesiastical Record 5S. XIII-338.

ors exercise themselves full ordinary jurisdiction in the diocese.[13] Whatever power therefore the law gives to the Ordinary is possessed at this time by the diocesan consultors acting of course *collegialiter*.

It is not the intention of the law however that either the chapter or the diocesan consultors exercise this jurisdiction themselves very long. Within eight days after obtaining certain notice of the vacancy the chapter and hence too the diocesan consultors must proceed to the election of the Vicar-capitular. These eight days[14] accept no interruption as no qualification is made here of a *tempus utile*.[15] Where the chapter handles also the revenues it must elect in addition to the Vicar-capitular a person called the procurator[16] but in this country at least at present the diocesan consultors do not handle the finances of the diocese and therefore need not elect this procurator.[17]

To enforce early appointment of a single administrator the Holy See limits this power of the chapter or the diocesan consultors to eight days after the knowledge of vacancy so that at the end of that time it devolves upon the metropolitan or the senor suffragan bishop to appoint the administrator. The canon states specifically that this devolves upon the bishop mentioned no matter what may have been the cause of the delay culpable or inculpable. The consultors therefore should exercise their prerogative as soon as they reasonably can after death and in the meantime they should notify the Holy See of the vacancy which has occurred. Parapraph 3 of this canon 432 refers to dioceses dependent directly upon the Holy See. We have no such dioceses in this country.

Who is to convoke the diocesan consultor we have studied in chapter VII under our remarks on precedence. It is the duty of the senior consultor to summon the other consultors and as the law specifies no peculiar method

13 Can. 198.
14 Can. 432.
15 Can. 35,
16 Can. 432.
17 Augustine, op. cit. II-482.

they may be summoned even by telephone although if some of the consultors are away at a distance they may be summoned by letter and time given them to appear. In the convocation the hour and the place of the meeting should of course be specified but if at any time all should be present accidentally even without convocation they could proceed to the election. In this election they are to follow absolutely the rules laid down in the New Code in art. II-*De electione*, cap. I, tit. IV, Lib. II. This is perhaps the only case among the secular clergy where these canons will apply in our country. Our statement in a previous chapter is to be recalled that these canons are to be held applicable in virtue of canon 20 even if one should deny that the consultors form a moral collegiate person.

In this article on election, passing over what has not direct application to our case, as for instance canon 161 which for our matter is modified by the requirements of canon 432 that the election take place within eight days, we should especially note canon 162. Note that failure to convoke one third of the number of consultors would invalidate the election. On the other hand it is not necessary to send the summons after them wherever they happen to be but it is sufficient to send it to the place of their domicile. This election must be strictly private and therefore no one no matter what his dignity cannot be admitted except the consultors of the diocese. Canon 167 might apply in case a consultor has in penalty been deprived of active voice, the other disabilities will be rare. The election moreover must take place by secret balloting. Election through "compromissum" or postulation will hardly occur in connection with the Vicar-capitular. It is to be noted that the one elected has eight days to answer whether he accepts the position or not. (Can. 175) The elect in this case does not require any confirmation and therefore immediately on his own acceptance he can exercise the functions of the office.

Besides the general provisions there are the particular provisions of canons 433-434 requiring for instance absolute majority. It is especially to be noted that the Vicar-capitular must be at least thirty years of age otherwise the election is null.

As soon as the Vicar-capitular is elected and has made the profession of faith all the ordinary power possessed by the diocesan consultors passes to him alone and after that moment the consultors return to their status of advisers only with the difference that in many cases the Vicar-capitular requires their consent where the bishop required only their advice. Thus we have already spoken of their consent required to permit the Vicar-capitular to appoint a substitute consultor.

It may happen that the Vicar-capitular will resign and then canon 443 is to be observed i. e. the chapter or the board of diocesan consultors must only be shown an authentic copy of his resignation and it is valid without their approval. The Holy See alone can remove a Vicar-capitular. The election of the new Vicar-capitular follows the same norms as the first election.

There are few additional duties of the diocesan consultors to be exercised by them *sede vacante.* The first one such in the New Code is the prescription of canon 113 in which the Vicar-capitular is permitted to excardinate or incardinate clerics but only after the vacancy has continued for a year and then with the *consent* of the board of consultors. This is only a general application of the principle *sede vacante nihil innovetur."* (Can. 436) Another similar legislation is that of canon 958 p. 1 n. 3 permitting the Vicar-capitular to grant dimissorial letters for ordaining clerics by another (or even by himself if himself a bishop). This power is contingent likewise upon the vacancy continuing for a year and requiring the *consent* of the consultors. There is however a new extension to this privilege. With the *consent* of the consultors the Vicar-capitular might even grant dimissorial letters within a year if there is some extraordinary need in the diocese. The reference to benefices in the canon is not new but the latter words of the same canon allowing use of this privilege to fill some important office will be of great help in this country. In both cases however the consultors must judge the gravity of the cause and give their consent accordingly.

More novel is the provision of canon 373 p. 5 permitting the Vicar-capitular to suspend or even remove from office the chancellor and similar diocesan officials. Here it must be borne in mind that the chancellor in the Code is scarcely more than a secretary. The important duties that by custom have been given him in this country are due to the chancellor being frequently appointed the Vicar-general whose duties however in that capacity cease the moment the see becomes vacant. This chancellor therefore and other notaries (e. g. notary in the matrimonial court) can be dismissed even by the Vicar-capitular but solely with the *consent* of the diocesan consultors who should be loath to give their consent unless there be some urgent cause.

This exhausts the additional duties of the consultors *sede vacante* in which their *consent* is required. There is however another new duty assigned to them in the New Code. The new legislation prescribes that in every diocesan chancery there be two safes for archives, one for the ordinary acts of the curia and another for the location of secret documents especially those belonging to criminal trials. The secrecy of this additional vault is safeguarded in the Code by many prescriptions and principally by this that there must be two separate keys to it kept by different persons, viz: the Bishop and the Vicar-general. Upon the vacancy of the see the Bishop's key passes into the possession of the Vicar-capitular but the other key must be given in our case to the consultor who is senior in the office. (Can. 381 p. 1). Nor is this all. During the vacancy this secret vault must be sealed and to open it during that time the Vicar-capitular requires some urgent cause and even then he must have two diocesan consultors present with him at the opening after which the vault must be sealed anew. There is moreover a penal sanction attached to any unlawful removing of a document from this secret vault, those guilty of this crime incurring an excommunication reserved to the Holy See. (Can. 2405.)

With this we end our study of the diocesan consultors. Briefly we found them a modern institution prospering chiefly in the United States and Australia and now by the New Code prescribed for all countries in similar conditions. We find the particular legislation in most points retained but in the New Code their duties are broadened and better defined and not impossibly they are now a moral collegiate person. Their greatest duty now is to elect the Administrator of the vacant diocese and in addition to the cases where the Bishop must call upon the consultors this Administrator must obtain their *consent* in four specific cases viz: 1) election of substitute consultor, 2) incardination and excardination, 3) granting dimissorials, and 4) the suspension or removal of minor diocesan officials. *Sede plena* their *consent* is required in two cases by common law i. e. in alienation and location (lease). Besides, their advice, always to be given *collegialiter* is required in the following instances. 1) In the union, transfer, division, dismemberment and penal suppression of benefices (parishes), 2) before entrusting a parish to the religious, 3) in the appointment of seminary deputies, 4) in the appointment and removal of synodal examiners and parish-priest consultors. 5) in determining the amount of suitable funeral offerings, 6) in determining the status of a new parish and to change a removable parish to an irremovable one. 7) episcopal reservations of sins, 8) in extraordinary public processions, 9) in determining the amount of offering for use of sacred vestments and utensils and finally 10) in the appointment of the members of the diocesan council of administration of church property. By Baltimore law still in force their advice will be required in this country additionally in 1) convoking a synod 2) in those cases of alienation where the Ordinaries apply their powers under the indult of the Holy See and 3) their advice may be taken in settling certain salary questions for the pastors. To all practical purposes they are the same as the cathedral chapter. The latter still probably is the Church's ideal but whether their introduction into this country at an early date is to be desired or not is not for the writer to settle. At present let the prescriptions of the Code be fully applied to them and in time these boards of diocesan consultors may be prepared for formal incorporation as cathedral chapters. We of the United States had a great part, perhaps the greatest, in the upbuilding of this institution of diocesan consultors; let us now retain the leadership and become the country in which the prescriptions of the Code in this matter are best observed.

APPENDIX.

We may mention here a council that under the law of the Code is to be established in every Vicariate and Prefecture-Apostolic. (Can. 302) This council mentioned already in the Collectanea Sacrae Congregationis de Propaganda Fide (II. p. 191, No. 7; ed. 1907) is to consist of at least three priests but it is not an incorporated body nor do they at all come under the provisions of the Code applying to diocesan consultors and hence have neither their rights nor their duties. The Code provides few duties for this council. These are 1) the duties of consultors in reference to the secret archives (can. 304), 2) their advice is required in removing a missionary (Can. 307 p. 2) and in appointing rectors of their quasi-parishes. (Can. 457) Other duties must be sought for in local legislation. The more advanced the mission the more desirable that by local legislation e. g. by synodal or provincial council's legislation their rights and duties be defined to approach as closely as possible the rights and duties of diocesan consultors. We have one vicariate-apostolic in the continental United States viz: in North Carolina and another in Alaska. The duties of the councils in those places are therefore to be regulated by their own local enactments. We doubt whether even the provisions of the Baltimore council would apply there.

BIBLIOGRAPHY.

SOURCES.

Acta Apostolicae Sedis. Romae, 1901.

Acta et Decreta Concilii Plenarii Australiensis II. Sydney, 1898.

Acta et Decreta Concilii Plenarii Australiensis III. Sydney, 1907.

Acta et Decreta Concilii Plenarii Baltimorensis II. Baltimorae, 1868.

Acta et Decreta Concilii Plenarii Baltimorensis III. Baltimorae, 1886.

Acta Pii X. Romae, 1905-1909.

Codex Iuris Canonici. Romae, 1918.

Collectanea Sacrae Congregationis de Propaganda Fide. Romae, 1907.

Collectio Lacensis, Acta et decreta conciliorum recentiorum. 1870 ss.

Concilii Tridentum, Friburgi Brisgoviae.

Concilium Plenarium Americae Latinae, Acta et Decreta, (1899) Romae, 1901.

Concilium Plenarium Sydneyense, Sydney, 1887.

Corpus Iuris Canonici. (Friedberg) Lipsiae, 1879-1881.

MANSI, *Amplissima Collectio Conciliorum. Parisiis,* 1901-1913.

Synodus Mobiliensis Prima (1835). Notre Dame University Press, Ed. 2, 1890.

BIBLIOGRAPHY.

American Catholic Quarterly Review. October 1878.

American Ecclesiastical Review.

American Ecclesiastical Review, The New Canon Law in its Practical Aspects. Phila. 1918.

AUGUSTINE, O. S. B., *A Commentary on Canon Law. St.* Louis, 1918-1919.

BAART, *Legal Formulary*, New York, 1898.

BAART, *The Roman Court*, New York, 1895.

BARGILLIAT, *Praelectiones Juris Canonici, Ed.* tricesima. Parisiis, 1915.

BLAT, O. P., *Commentarium Textus Codicis Iuris Canonici.* Romae, 1919.

CATHOLIC ENCYCLOPEDIA, Art. "Consultors Diocesan", etc.

Canoniste contemporain (Le), periodical, Paris, 1878-ss.

CASTILLO, *Disertacion sobre la potestad del Cabildo en Sede Vacante* etc.

CREAGH, The Code of Canon Law and the Church in U. S. Catholic University, Washington.

FERRERES, *Institutiones Canonicae*, Barcinone, 1917

GIGNAC, *Compendium Juris Canonici.* Quebec, 1913.

Irish Ecclesiastical Record.

Metropolitan Catholic Directory, 1854. Baltimore.

NILLES, S. J., *Commentaria in Concilium Plenarium Baltimorense III*, Oeniponte, 1890.

ORBIS CATHOLICUS, 1918, London.

Official Catholic Directory, (Kenedy) 1919. New York.

PAPI, S. J., *The Government of Religious Communities.* New York, 1919.

Sadlier's Catholic Directory, 1866, New York.

SHEA, *The Catholic Church in Colonial Days.* New York, 1886.

SHEA, *The Life and Times of Archbishop Carroll.* New York, 1888.

SHEA, *History of the Catholic Church in the United States.* 1808-1866.

SMITH, *Elements of Ecclesiastical Law.* 9-th edition. New York, 1893.

SMITH, *Notes on the Second Plenary Council of Baltimore.* New York, 1874.

TAUNTON, *Law of the Church,* London, 1906.
TRUDEL, *Dictionary of Canon Law.* St. Louis, 1919.
VERMEERSH S. J. CREUSEN S. J., *Summa Novi Juris Canonici commentariis aucta.*
WERNZ, *Ius Decretalium.* Tomus II. ed. tertia, Prati, 1915. Tomus III ed. prima. Romae, 1901.
ZITELLI, Apparatus Juris Ecclesiastici, ed. altera, Romae, 1888.

DEUS LUX MEA

CANONES

QUOS

AD DOCTORATUS GRADUM

IN

JURE CANONICO

APUD UNIVERSITATEM CATHOLICAM

AMERICAE CONSEQUENDUM

PUBLICE PROPUGNABIT

PETRUS JOANNES KLEKOTKA

SACERDOS ARCHIDIOECESIS

PHILADELPHIENSIS JURIS CANONICI

LICENTIATUS

Hora IX A. M. Die III. Junii, A. D. MCMXX

Universitas Catholica Americae
Washington, D. C.
Sacra Facultas Theologica
1919-1920
No. 8

CANONES

I. Canones 1-7, 8-24. (De legibus ecclesiasticis).
II. " 25-20. (De consuetudine).
III. " 36-62. (De rescriptis).
IV. " 63-79. (De privilegiis).
V. " 80-86. (De dispensationibus).
VI. " 91-95. (De domicilio et quasi-domicilio)
VII. " 1, 98, 756, 866, 1097 p. 2. (De ritibus).
VIII. " 99-102. (De personis moralibus).
IX. " 111-117. (De clericorum adscriptione).
X. " 160-178. (De electione).
XI. " 183-195. (De amissione officiorum ecclesiasticorum).
XII. " 196-210. (De potestate ordinaria et delegata).
XIII. " 246-257. (De Sacris Congregationibus).
XIV. " 258-259, 1597-1605. (De Tribunalibus Curiae Romanae).
XV. " 281-292. (De Conciliis plenariis et provincialibus).
XVI. " 350-355. (De Coadjutoribus et Auxiliaribus Episcoporum).
XVII. " 356-362. (De Synodo dioecesana).
XVIII. " 363-390. (De Curia dioecesana).
XIX. " 423-428. (De consultoribus dioecesanis).
XX. " 429-444. (De sede impedita aut vacante ac de Vicario Capiaulari).
XXI. " 451-470. (De parochis).
XXII. " 471-478. (De vicariis paroecialibus).

XXIII. " 518-530. (De confessariis et capellanis religiosorum).
XXIV. " 684-699. (De fidelium associationibus in genere).
XXV. " 824-844. (De Missarum eleemosynis seu stipendiis).
XXVI. " 871-892. (De ministro sacramenti poenitentiae).
XXVII. " 893-900. (De reservatione peccatorum).
XXVIII. " 911-936. (De indulgentiis).
XXIX. " 951-967. (De ministro sacrae ordinationis).
XXX. " 1019-1034. (De iis quae matrimonii celebrationi praemitti debent).
XXXI. " 1043-1057. (De dispensationibus matrimonialibus).
XXXII. Canon 1069. (De impedimento ligaminis).
XXXIII. Canones 1070-1071. (De impedimento disparitatis cultus).
XXXIV. " 97, 1077. (De impedimento affinitatis).
XXXV. Canon 1078. (De impedimento publicae honestatis).
XXXVI. Canones 1059, 1080. (De impedimento cognationis legalis).
XXXVII. " 1081-1093. (De consensu matrimoniali).
XXXVIII. " 1094-1103. (De forma celebrationis matrimonii).
XXXIX. " 1118-1127. (De dissolutione vinculi).
XL. " 1133-1137. (De convalidatione simplici).
XLI. " 1161-1187. (De ecclesiis).
XLII. " 1215-1238. (De cadaveris translatione ad ecclesiam, funere ac depositione).
XLIII. " 1307-1315. (De voto).

XLIV.	"	1337-1348. (De sacris concionibus).
XLV.	"	1395-1405. (De prohibitione librorum).
XLVI.	"	1409-1412. (De notione beneficii ecclesiastici).
XLVII.	"	1414-1418. (De constitutione sue erectione beneficiorum).
XLVIII.	"	1419-1430. (De unione, translatione, divisione, dismembratione, conversione et suppressione beneficiorum.
XLIX.	"	1472-1483 (De juribus et obligationibus beneficiatorum).
L.	"	1556-1568. (De foro competenti).
LI.	"	1960-1992. (De causis matrimonialibus).
LII.	"	2147-2161. (De modo procedendi in remotione parochorum).
LIII.	"	2162-2167. (De modo procedendi in translatione parochorum).
LIV.	"	2186-2194 (De modo procedeni in suspensione ex informata conscientia infligenda).
LV.	"	2226-2235. (De subjecto coactivae potestati obnoxio).
LVI.	"	2241-2254, 2237 p. 2 (De censuris in genere).
LVII.	"	2257-2267. (De excommunicatione).
LVIII.	"	2268-2277. (De interdicto).
LIX.	"	2278-2285. (De suspensione).
LX.	"	2286-2305. (De poenis vindicativis).

Vidit Sacra Facultas:

Joannes A. Ryan, S.T.D., p. t. Decanus.
Petrus Guilday, Ph.D., p. t. a Secretis.
Vidit Rector Universitatis,
+Thomas J. Shahan, S.T.D., J.U.L., LL.D.

www.ingramcontent.com/pod-product-compliance
Lightning Source LLC
LaVergne TN
LVHW050230080826
844660LV00012B/508
9780813221991